EDUCATION: Planning and Human Development

EDUCATION

Planning and Human Development

(In 8 Volumes)

Education: A Key to Development

(Volume 1)

V.C. PANDEY

ISHA BOOKS
DELHI—110 033

EDUCATION: Planning and Human Development

(Education)

Rs. 7000 (Set in 8 Vols.)

ISBN: 81-8205-006-5 (Set)
ISBN: 81-8205-007-3 (Vol. 1)

Published in 2003 in India by
Isha Books, D-43, Prithviraj Road
Adarsh Nagar, Delhi-110 033

Lasertypesetting by: Varsha Graphics, Delhi
Printed at: Chawla Offset Press, Delhi

Preface

The importance of education in the life of a nation and the rise of civilisation cannot be underestimated. Education has always been necessary to preserve the human race from a lapse into rude ignorance. It is the medium by which civilisation is preserved and fostered. It is, therefore, both a tool and a virtue. It is essential to the preservation of tradition, the perpetuation of the accumulated learning and experience of past generations, the training of persons of learning and expertise in various essential fields and the communication of discoveries and inventions. Above all, it equips individuals for the prudent conduct of their lives.

Education does not aim at the mechanical reproduction of subjective views. In the context of the inherent limitations of the human mind, education aims and reaches towards a concept of truth and the development of faculties of objective assessment. It relies upon the propensity for truth to prevail through objective enquiry, discussion, analysis, appreciation and discrimination. Truth and objectivity in an absolute sense are unachievable by human beings, but what is crucial is to strive towards the ideal with an awareness of human imperfections.

True education is beneficial to personal development in many ways. It assists a person to rise above banality and sordidity, lifting him out of cultural barbarism and acquainting him with civilised culture. It illuminates his mind with learning, the thought and experience of generations uncounted. Giving him knowledge it helps him to understand the world, his place and his duties. It helps him to rise above his circumstances, even adversity, to master his destiny.

The incidence of education of a high standard is a mark of a civilised nation. It is both a contributing factor towards and a result of, such eminence. It helps to prdduce responsible, productive, prudent, creative and erudite citizens. It is necessary for the preservation of knowledge and tradition and to the processes of constructive technological and institutional development. However, it is only true education that can further these objects. The substitution of a system founded upon false principles can only be destructive of the general welfare, since it undermines the benefits and virtues that true education conveys and that are necessary to the maintenance of civil standards.

Editor

Contents

1

Education in Societal Diversification

Education is a fundamental human right. It provides children, youth and adults with the power to reflect, make choices and enjoy a better life. It breaks the cycle of poverty and is a key ingredient in economic and social development.

The increasing diversity within the schools is also demonstrated by the higher visibility of other groups of diverse learners, including, but not limited to, children with disabilities, children and families identified with the deaf culture, and gay and lesbian youth. The challenges in working with an ever growing pluralistic school population encompass many areas.

The provision of relevant multicultural curriculums, the use of culturally sensitive assessment and intervention strategies, the training of school staff in the provision of these services, the recruitment and retention of multicultural and diverse professionals, and the integration of diverse communities and parents in an authentic and empowering manner are only a few of the critical issues facing those working with today's students.

Professionals are also challenged by the need to consider the impact of complex social/environmental problems, which in many contexts have negative consequences for children from various racial/ethnic and social class backgrounds. Although there has clearly been a greater recognition of the need for training in multicultural competence across professions, many programs still conceptualize this training as more of an "add-on"; that is, programs require only one or two courses for their particular professional specialty.

This is in contrast to a more comprehensive and integrated "paradigm shift" in the teaching of all helping professional courses. The training of school staff and other related professionals can be conceptualized by using a model that emphasizes three major components: awareness, knowledge, and skills.

The awareness component involves professionals examining their own values, myths, stereotypes, and world view. Knowledge entails developing a non-stereotyping, flexible understanding of cultural, social, and family dynamics of diverse groups, along with a comprehension of the critical sociopolitical, historical, and economic contexts in which people from diverse multicultural groups are embedded.

Skills require the development of culturally sensitive, flexible, and empowering treatment and assessment strategies that are accompanied by communication skills, the integration of multicultural and diversity issues in various treatment modalities, multicultural consultation, and advocacy skills.

Depending on the school, staff, and community context, flexible training can take place on many levels, such as formal multicultural issues course work, in-service training, long-term consultation and analysis, multicultural program development, and reciprocal relationships with the surrounding multicultural communities. A useful model that allows for the integration of many of these critical variables is the Ecological Model developed by Bronfenbrenner and enhanced by others.

According to this model, we try to understand or evaluate a student (the microsystem) in the context of his/her mesosystems (immediate family, extended family, friends, network), macrosystems (culture or subculture), and exosystems (social structures). This model places the diverse learner, school staff, and parents/community in an ecological context, which then allows both for a broader understanding of the critical issues affecting students from diverse backgrounds and the development of relevant service and educational models.

These educational models need to be highly sensitive to the particular community and social contexts of which the diverse learners and school staff are members. For the diverse learner and the school staff, the ability to conceptualize and integrate culture and issues of diversity within a developmental perspective is also crucial, given the changes in developmental tasks at each life stage and the various ways that these "tasks" are expressed and resolved within various cultural groups. Relevant to the diverse learner in schools, these issues must be integrated within the specialized early intervention programs offered to children with developmental issues.

Early intervention services are an extremely important part of the total, life-stage conceptualization for low income, diverse learners because such learners are more vulnerable to developmental concerns. Through the development of multicultural competencies within the areas of awareness, knowledge, and skills, the probability increases of psychologists using assessment and treatment strategies that meet the needs of a wide range of culturally diverse groups.

The need for flexible and culturally sensitive assessment techniques has continued to be stressed by many in the field. Examinations of the critical features in assessment should include the sociocultural context of the diverse learner and his family, the sociocultural background of the examiner, such as issues of awareness of biases and stereotypes, and the selection of appropriate testing, interview, and survey instruments. All of these measures enhance the possibility of more relevant and culturally sensitive assessments.

Furthermore, the consideration of issues related to language and its complexities is another major factor in providing relevant and meaningful assessments. The need for changes in the conceptualization of children's abilities and how skills are assessed, particularly with diverse learners, has also led to strategies that focus on problem-solving abilities. Maker, Nielson, and Rogers described the need for change in assessments within a diverse school settings, including the assessments of students who are to be considered "gifted." These procedures stress the process of problem solving and they offer an examination of each child's pattern of multiple intelligences in an attempt to get away from the more traditional and, at times, rigid analyses based on formal intelligence and skills testing.

Likewise, the model of Maker, Nielson, and Rogers has great implications for the assessment of children of all levels and children from diverse backgrounds. Their model allows for individual analyses of children's particular problem-solving style and strengths, which are then encouraged, while areas for remediation are addressed. Intervention strategies also need to incorporate the critical issues of culture and social context.

Works on specific cultural groups, such as Lock on interventions with African American youth, Jackson on counseling youth of Arab Ancestry, Thomason on counseling Native American clients, Zapata on working with Latinos, and Yagi & Oh on interventions with Asian American youth, provide valuable guidelines on working with specific populations and serve to increase awareness of the specific cultural factors relevant to that particular cultural group. Awareness of, and the ability to assess, specific factors such as acculturation, language proficiency (including guidelines on the use of translators), and sociocultural history, further enhances the provision of culturally affirming treatment strategies.

The need to deal with diverse groups must also include work with gay and lesbian youth and youth with disabilities, particularly as we proceed with educational inclusion models which are further enhancing the diversity presented within school systems. With the changing composition of today's student population, the need to provide educational programs that address the complex issues related to multiculturalism and diversity is becoming more and more evident.

Schools and educators must begin to develop curriculums that integrate awareness, knowledge, and skills within educational materials. It is critical that diversity and multiculturalism not be conceived as being accomplished by adding a course, a lecture, or a one-day "multicultural fair." A total curriculum transformation needs to take place where the critical issues of diversity and multiculturalism are integrated into all aspects of students' academic achievement, social skills development, and relationship with the community at large. An example of such an attempt is the work of one of the authors who developed a psycho-educational course to help students increase their self-awareness, acceptance and appreciation of the self and others, and communication skills. The course was tried in two multicultural schools and in one school comprised mainly of minority children.

The response from the students and teachers of both regular and special education classrooms was positive. They noticed the nurturing climate developed through the course. The opportunity for children to begin to integrate into their lives issues related to multiculturalism and diversity is vital to the development of acceptance and respect for others from diverse backgrounds. Along with traditional educational models that present historical and social information about people from diverse backgrounds, the creation of models that stress the development of awareness and cultural sensitivity skills needs to take place.

Under this general category of enhancing multicultural awareness and respect for diversity is the critical need for confronting issues of racism and prejudice. Another major component in working with diverse learners is that of establishing "authentic" relationships with parents and the community. This is a critical element of any effort directed towards increasing multicultural understanding and the development of a truly pluralistic school and community environment. To become actively involved in school is hard for immigrant parents who are not familiar with American school systems.

Workshops on American schools including structure, rules, services, and the rights and responsibilities of parents and children are found to be helpful, even empowering, to these parents. The need for direct work with parents and communities has been stressed by Atkinson and Juntunen: "... school personnel must function as a school-home-community liaison, as an interface between school and home, school and community, and home and community".

Casas & Furlong, writing with regards to Hispanic parents, but offering ideas clearly applicable to other multicultural groups, stress the advocacy role of school counselors both to "...increase parent participation and facilitate the increase empowerment..." of parents and the community.

This is a critical role that needs to be taken on not just by school counselors, but by all school staff working with diverse learners in an increasingly multicultural environment. In short, learners from diverse multicultural groups, children with disabilities, and gay and lesbian youth will continue to present challenges to schools and those providing educational and support services. The development of educational curriculums that enhance awareness, knowledge, and skills for students is vital if schools are to provide culturally relevant, respectful, and affirming teaching environments.

To that end, the development of culturally sensitive assessment and intervention strategies, multicultural consultation, and professional training needs to take place. Structured along the lines of awareness, knowledge, and skills development, such actions will enhance diversity within the school environment. The diverse student and community can be conceptualized as a wonderful and exciting element of the world we live in, and not as a hindrance to the educational process.

The authentic involvement of parents as active and empowered members of the school community will link school staff with the diverse learner, further increasing and affirming cultural diversity within our school settings

In adult English as a second language (ESL) and family ESL literacy classrooms, learners' ways of understanding and acting in the world may differ radically from those of the mainstream population. Educators respect and honour their learners' "ways of knowing" when they create and work from curricula that emerge from issues of importance to them.

However, too often teachers let their learners' knowledge and views of the world slip by unnoticed. When learners' ways of understanding the world are not heard and accepted, everyone loses—the learners, who bring this knowledge with them to schools; the parents, who want to pass on cultural traditions but find themselves fighting both the school information and their children's perceptions of the value of their own cultural beliefs; and the teachers, who could be opening new worlds of exploration to children and themselves while providing a bridge between the culture of the school and the culture of the home.

In effective family ESL literacy programs—where literacy needs of children and their parents are addressed through instruction in English, native language literacy, cross-cultural development, self-esteem, family learning, and home school relations diverse ways of knowing are explored and valued. In these programs, it is especially important that learning be multi- directional: Children, parents, and teachers all learn from one another as they share their experiences.

For example, some family literacy projects use elders' storytelling as a basis for lessons. Other projects encourage children to discuss and value their cultural traditions and family routines. Elementary school educators and researchers have done much to inform the field about the importance of valuing families' ways of knowing.

One research study shows that classroom practice can be "developed, transformed, and enriched" when researchers and teachers who have received training in interviewing techniques visit minority student households to discover the "historically developed and accumulated strategies (skills, abilities, ideas, practices) or bodies of knowledge that are essential to a household's functioning and well-being". In participatory adult ESL programs, teachers conduct informal research in the classroom itself using dialogue journals, family trees, life journeys, class newspapers, and speaking and writing assignments from learners' photos.

Designed to elicit issues and concerns of importance to learners, these activities also serve to uncover learners' ways of knowing the world. One example of such an activity comes from a program for American Indian parents in Minnesota. Learners demonstrate the richness of their alternative knowledge by comparing parenting styles and family values of Indian parents to those of mainstream culture.

In short, in adult ESL and ESL family literacy programs, teachers can provide cultural and linguistic bridges to connect the worlds of the home and the classroom by recognizing, honouring, and building on students' ways of looking at and understanding the world and by building curricula and classroom learning around this knowledge.

Development of Career Education

In US, census data show rapid increases in nonwhite populations, a vast reserve of human potential that makes a multicultural focus imperative for career education and development. Wurzel defines multicultural perspective as a critical and reflective understanding of oneself and others in historical and cultural contexts, an awareness of both differences and human similarities.

For career educators and counselors, it means infusing practice with an awareness of their own personal and cultural background and experiences as well as those of their students or clients. Self-concept and identity are crucial to career development.

Cultural values and beliefs have great influence on the formation of self-concept; therefore, effective career development must take culture into account. The purpose of multicultural career education and development is to foster positive self-concepts and career choices regardless of cultural background, encourage understanding of the contributions of all cultural groups, and develop effective intercultural communication skills. World view—the attitudes, values, opinions, and beliefs with which a person perceives the world—is influenced by cultural heritage and life experiences.

Locke and Parker explain how different combinations of Locus of Control (LC) and Locus of Responsibility (LR) affect the formation of world view. Four combinations are as follows:

- *Internal LC-Internal LR*—feelings of high personal control and personal attributions of success or failure;
- *External LC-Internal LR*—acceptance of the dominant culture's definition of self-responsibility;
- *External LC-External LR*—feelings of a lack of both control and responsibility; and
- *Internal LC-External LR*—belief in individual efficacy but perceptions of external barriers to action.

The category that corresponds with an individual's world view derives from his/her cultural background as well as the historical, social, and economic experience of that cultural group. This is the context in which students will attempt to act on their career choices. One of the dangers of multiculturalism is thinking that all members of a group share identical characteristics.

However, cultural awareness must begin with understanding of such differences as world view, bearing in mind that people are a complex product of gender, ethnicity, and individuality. Another dimension of difference is nonverbal communication styles.

Interpretations of words, gestures, spatial and temporal relationships, and touch can vary among groups. Other values and perspectives on which groups may differ are as follows: cause and effect, holistic versus linear thinking, competition versus harmony, long- versus short-term goals, view of the teacher or counselor as authority or facilitator, collectivism versus individualism, degree of tolerance for ambiguity, assertiveness versus restraint, and authoritarian versus democratic family structures. Intercultural communication means the ability to approximate another person's meanings, without necessarily agreeing with them.

A culturally effective career educator has a wide repertoire of skills to interpret the world views and communication styles of students and to select the best strategies and techniques to help them. An El Paso, Texas, project provides an example. Hispanic females have high dropout rates and the lowest college attendance rate of any ethnic population.

The alienation of many Latinas from school stems from lack of role models and counseling, stereotypes in curriculum, and low teacher expectations. Mothers are a strong influence, but many mothers have low educational levels and lower expectations for their daughters.

The Mother-Daughter Program jointly operated by the University of Texas, the YWCA, and El Paso School District builds on the strong maternal influence. Sixth-grade girls and their mothers participate in a program designed to acquaint them with careers and college, raise aspirations, introduce them to Hispanic female role models, and help mothers to be role models.

The program targets sixth-graders because it is felt that the pre-high school period is a critical time before girls conform to cultural norms and restrict their own options. Program activities include campus tours, career day, community service projects, awards ceremonies, and summer camp, a 2-day immersion in campus life. An important factor in the program's success is respect for the participants' language (using bilingual materials) and cultural traits.

A key to effective career education and development for diverse groups is the sensitivity and awareness of educators and counselors. Locke and Parker describe the cross-cultural awareness continuum, which educators and counselors can use to gauge their growth in intercultural competence, a lifelong, ongoing process. The levels of the continuum are: i) Self-awareness ii) Awareness of one's own culture iii) Awareness of racism, sexism, and poverty iv) Awareness of individual differences v) Awareness of other cultures vi) Awareness of diversity vii) Career education skills/techniques.

Culturally skilled career counselors or educators are aware of their own ethnicity and personal prejudices, have knowledge and understanding of culturally diverse groups, and have knowledge of culturally relevant strategies, skills, materials, and resources. Examples of a secondary and a postsecondary program illustrate ways of integrating multicultural techniques.

The Iowa Department of Public Instruction's approach to secondary multicultural career education begins with the premise that students must see themselves reflected in the curriculum and must see the potential for themselves in various careers. The curriculum has five parts:

— self-concept (including race, sex, national origin, and physical condition);

— understanding of the world of work;

— understanding of the contributions of all groups to society;

— commonalities of the human race, uniqueness of individuals and cultural groups; and

— interpersonal and intergroup communication.

The following strategies synthesize from a number of sources some approaches to multicultural career education/development:

Teachers and counselors should establish a climate of acceptance, have high expectations for student achievement, and foster positive self-concepts and cultural identity. A cultural group should not be thought of as homogeneous. For example, Asians are composed of many different subgroups.

Native American differences appear among tribes, in urban and rural environments, and intergenerationally. Teachers should strive for a balanced view of students as individuals and group members. Curriculum materials should be representative of all groups in a wide range of careers.

Bilingualism should be valued and students' language and culture incorporated in instruction. Students should be helped to learn the difference between feelings of superiority and pride in one's heritage.

Reflective teaching practices and sharing of the teacher's own ethnicity and background can foster a sense of community. Differences in communication styles, learning styles, and decision-making styles should be assessed and appropriate teaching and counseling methods selected.

Although a goal of career development is empowering people to change their lives, a focus solely on individual competence ignores the effects of external forces.

Teachers and counselors are encouraged to be advocates for students by recognizing problems that are systemic rather than individual. Acting as change agents, they can seek commitment from administrators for a multicultural perspective, examine institutional practices and the values they represent, and question the assumed universality of theories, methods, and instruments used in career development.

Lee and Richardson recognize the potential of counselors as systemic change agents but identify some concerns about an overbroad definition of multiculturalism and the potential for a new kind of racism by overemphasis on differences. They present the following considerations for a multicultural approach:

a) The importance of a group's history, the way its perspective is derived from exclusion from power

b) The level of ethnic identity and acculturation

c) Influence of family, sex role socialization, and religion

d) The way a group has been named or labeled

e) Some groups' traditional mistrust of counseling and education as tools of social control

Locke and Parker conclude that system commitment to meaningful career education, a belief that students can learn and want to learn, and educators and counselors who value the worth and dignity of all students are the keys to successful multicultural career development.

Multiculturalism has been defined as the fourth force in psychology, one which complements the psychodynamic, behavioural and humanistic explanations of human behaviour. Pedersen defined multiculturalism as "a wide range of multiple groups without grading, comparing, or ranking them as better or worse than one another and without denying the very distinct and complementary or even contradictory perspectives that each group brings with it". Regardless of how one defines the term or the degree to which the concept is restricted or broadened in a particular context, multiculturalism encompasses a world of complex detail.

There are four dimensions of cultures. These dimensions are:

1) Power distance—the extent to which a culture accepts that power in institutions and organizations is distributed unequally.

2) Uncertainty avoidance—the extent to which members of a culture feel threatened by uncertain or ambiguous situations.

3) Individualism—a social framework in which people are supposed to take care of themselves and of their immediate families only. Collectivism refers to a social framework in which people distinguish between in-groups and out-groups, expecting their in-group to look after them, and in exchange for that owe loyalty to it.

4) Masculinity/Femininity—the extent to which the dominant values within a culture are assertiveness, money and things, caring for others, quality of life, and people.

A number of generic counselor characteristics are necessary, but not sufficient, for those who engage in multicultural counseling. To be effective, a counselor must be able to: express respect for the client in a manner that is felt, understood, accepted, and appreciated by the client.

Respect may be communicated either verbally or nonverbally with voice quality or eye contact. Feel and express empathy for culturally different clients. This involves being able to place oneself in the place of the other, to understand the point of view of the other.

Personalize his/her observations. This means that the counselor recognizes that his/her observations, knowledge, or perceptions are "right" or "true" only for him/herself and that they do not generalize to the client. Withhold judgment and remain objective until one has enough information and an understanding of the world of the client.

Tolerate ambiguity refers to the ability to react to new, different, and at times, unpredictable situations with little visible discomfort or irritation. Have patience and perseverance when unable to get things done immediately. Counselors bring with them their own degree of effectiveness with these generic characteristics. They also bring with them their cultural manifestations as well as their unique personal, social and psychological background.

These factors interact with the cultural and personal factors brought by the client. The interaction of these two sets of factors must be explored along with other counseling-related considerations for each client who comes for counseling. The effective counselor is one who can adapt the counseling models, theories, or techniques to the unique individual needs of each client.

This skill requires that the counselor be able to see the client as both an individual and as a member of a particular cultural group. Multicultural counseling requires the recognition of:

— the importance of racial/ethnic group membership on the socialization of the client;

— the importance of and the uniqueness of the individual;

— the presence of and place of values in the counseling process; and

— the uniqueness of learning styles, vocational goals, and life purposes of clients, within the context of principles of democratic social justice.

The Multicultural Awareness Continuum was designed to illustrate the areas of awareness through which a counselor must go in the process of counseling a culturally different client. The continuum is linear and the process is developmental, best understood as a lifelong process.

Self-understanding is a necessary condition before one begins the process of understanding others. Both intrapersonal and interpersonal dynamics must be considered as important components in the projection of beliefs, attitudes, opinions, and values.

The examination of one's own thoughts and feelings allows the counselor a better understanding of the cultural "baggage" he or she brings to the situation. Counselors bring cultural baggage to the counseling situation; baggage that may cause certain things to be taken for granted or create expectations about behaviors and manners.

For example, consider your own name and the meaning associated with it. Ask yourself the cultural significance of your name. Could your name have some historical significance to cultures other than the culture of your origin? There may be some relationship between your name and the order of your birth. There may have been a special ceremony conducted when you were named. The naming process of a child is but one of the many examples of how cultural influences are evident and varied.

Language is specific to one's cultural group whether formal, informal, verbal, or nonverbal. Language determines the cultural networks in which an individual participates and contributes specific values to the culture. Racism, sexism, and poverty are all aspects of a culture that must be understood from the perspective of how one views their effect both upon oneself and upon others.

The words themselves are obviously powerful terms and frequently evoke some defensiveness. Even when racism and sexism are denied as a part of one's personal belief system, one must recognize that he/she never-the-less exists as a part of the larger culture.

Even when the anguish of poverty is not felt personally, the counselor must come to grips with his or her own beliefs regarding financially less fortunate people. Exploration of the issues of racism, sexism, and poverty may be facilitated by a "systems" approach. Such an exploration may lead to examination of the differences between individual behaviors and organizational behaviors, or what might be called the difference between personal prejudice and institutional prejudice.

The influence of organizational prejudice can be seen in the attitudes and beliefs of the system in which the counselor works. Similarly, the awareness that frequently church memberships exist along racial lines, or that some social organizations restrict their membership to one sex, should help counselors come to grips with the organizational prejudice which they may be supporting solely on the basis of participation in a particular organization.

One of the greatest pitfalls of the novice counselor is to overgeneralize things learned about a specific culture as therefore applicable to all members of the culture.

A single thread of commonality is often presumed to exist as interwoven among the group simply because it is observed in one or a few member(s) of the culture. On the contrary, cultural group membership does not require one to sacrifice individualism or uniqueness. Total belief in individualism fails to take into account the "collective family-community" relationship which exists in many cultural groups.

A real danger lies in the possibility that counselors may unwittingly discount cultural influences and subconsciously believe they understand the culturally different when, in fact, they view others from their own culture's point of view. In practice, what is put forth as a belief in individualism can become a disregard for any culturally specific behaviors that influence client behaviors.

In sum, counselors must be aware of individual differences and come to believe in the uniqueness of the individual before moving to the level of awareness of other cultures. Most cross-cultural emphasis is currently placed upon African Americans, Native Americans, Mexican Americans or Hispanics, and Asian Americans.

Language is of great significance and uniqueness to each of these cultural groups, rendering standard English less than complete in communication of ideas. It is necessary for counselors to be sensitive to words which are unique to a particular culture as well as body language and other nonverbal behaviors to which cultural significance is attached. The culture of the United States has often been referred to as a "melting pot." This characterization suggests that people came to the United States from many different countries and blended into one new culture.

Thus, old world practices were altered, discarded, or maintained within the context of the new culture. For the most part, many cultural groups did not fully participate in the melting pot process. The final level on the continuum is to implement what has been learned about working with culturally different groups and add specific techniques to the repertoire of counseling skills.

Before a counselor can effectively work with clients of diverse cultural heritage, he or she must have developed general competence as a counselor. Passage through the awareness continuum constitutes professional growth and will contribute to an increase in overall counseling effectiveness, but goes much further than that. Counselors must be aware of learning theory and how theory relates to the development of psychological-cultural factors.

Counselors must understand the relationship between theory and counselors' strategies or practices. Most importantly, counselors must have developed a sense of worth in their own cultures before attaining competence in counseling the culturally different.

Perhaps two of the most important changes within counseling and counselor education in the past twenty years have been (a) recognition of the need for a multicultural perspective in all aspects of counseling and education and (b) the evolution of supervision models and practices.

Recently, these changes culminated in two sets of competency and standards statements that will most certainly guide counselor preparation and evaluation of counselor practice.

The Association for Multicultural Counseling and Development (AMCD) approved a document outlining multicultural counseling competencies and standards and the Association for Counselor Education and Supervision (ACES), adopted comprehensive standards for eleven aspects of counseling supervision.

Now counselors are recognizing the need to consider multicultural issues in supervision and methods of multicultural supervision. The multicultural perspective will become essential as we move into the twenty-first century. It is projected that by the year 2010 twelve of our most populous states, containing about half of the nation's young people, will have significant minority populations.

Thus, the supervision triad of client, counselor, and supervisor will most likely contain persons of differing racial-ethnic backgrounds who are confronting problems and concerns in a diverse social environment. The supervisor is responsible for assuring that multicultural issues receive attention in supervision.

Generally, whenever the client is a minority group member, and sometimes when either the supervisee or supervisor is a minority person, supervisors will recognize the relevance of addressing cultural concerns.

However, all counseling and supervision contacts have cultural, racial-ethnic aspects which shape core assumptions, attitudes, and values of the persons involved and which may enhance or impede counselor effectiveness.

Logical extensions of this view of multicultural supervision are models that advocate supervision as a method to assist multicultural counselor development. These models propose that supervisees move in stages from minimal racial-ethnic awareness, to awareness of discrepancies between cultures and within self, and then to development of a multicultural identity. The supervisor's role is to promote supervisee growth by challenging cultural assumptions, encouraging emotional expression, and validating conflict of attitudes and values.

These multicultural models lack empirical support, but seem to integrate well with developmental models of supervision and direct the supervisor to assess the multicultural awareness level of each supervisee. A number of supervision techniques have been proposed to insure that the cultural dimension is addressed, though none have research support.

Planned discussion of culture and the culture of counseling; exploration of supervisee and supervisor cultural backgrounds; required use of videotape; modeling by the supervisor; inclusion of cultural considerations on all intake, case management, and other written supervision reports; and experiential exercises are methods that can be used in individual and group supervision.

All supervision is some form of multicultural supervision, supervisors will need to be proficient in the multicultural competencies. All supervisors-in-training should work with supervisees from racial-ethnic groups other than their own and receive supervision of multicultural supervision.

Social Cohesion

The education system, therefore, has a key role to play in fostering emotionally healthy children. The focus can no longer be exclusively be on academic concerns. A holistic approach must be adopted in the education of young persons in the region if the system is to contribute to the promotion of social cohesion and the reduction of levels of societal violence. A holistic approach to delivery of education implies that the role of the teacher has to be perceived very differently from what has been traditionally accepted.

The issue of responsible sexual behaviour, for example, not included here, is of paramount importance in today's world. However, the elements highlighted constitute an indispensable core for moulding the personalities of socially and emotionally well-adjusted young persons who, embodied with these characteristics, will be centres of inner calm and who will not only promote social cohesion, but will be predisposed to achieve personal success in whatever field of endeavour they choose to pursue. Loving yourself implies accepting yourself as you are, warts included, while taking active measures to change those personal characteristics that you deem in need of being changed. One who does not love self is incapable of loving anyone else.

Self-hate is the antithesis of self-love. It is intimately linked with personal insecurity and lack of self-confidence and is usually the cumulative result of systematic mistreatment in early childhood. Someone who is overwhelmed with self-hate is capable of doing an enormous amount of societal damage, including the perpetration of overt forms of violence.

Learning to disagree with someone else's point of view and yet respect it as valid is the basis for nurturing a culture of tolerance in society. This also provides a basis for respecting and accepting persons from different cultures. Teaching young persons to trust their own thinking is a big challenge for parents and the educational authorities. It is so easy instead to teach them to trust the thinking of the authority figure. But this is a trap because it serves to erode self-reliance, making it easy for such persons to be led astray by strong personalities who indulge in antisocial behaviour.

When young people, particularly young males, feel a sense of powerlessness and alienation, they are likely to promote disharmony in society. If what transpires in the classroom contributes to making the students feel a sense of powerlessness, this is likely be counterproductive to fostering social cohesion and a culture of nonviolence.

Conversely, if the classroom atmosphere is one of partnership between teacher and students, rather than a power relationship in which the teacher is seen as the authoritarian figure, this is likely to facilitate the development of self-confidence and social responsibility among the students. It ought to be self-evident that the use of corporal punishment as a sanction in the school system is quite inappropriate, because it is simply impossible to promote a culture of nonviolence through the use of violence.

In many countries of the region, guidance counsellors are attached to schools. One of the main aspects of their function is to interact with students who manifest behavioural problems. Their function is usually conducted outside of the normal classroom activities where the students interact with teachers teaching the various subject disciplines.

Although the 'fire fighting' role of guidance counsellors is important, what is even more critical is that teachers function as counsellors in their normal classroom interaction with their students. Functioning as counsellor in the classroom simply means that the teacher adopts as a norm a nurturing, pupil-enhancing posture where every child is treated with full respect, is listened to attentively and is perceived as valuable and capable of learning.

It is such an environment that is most conducive to young students learning to love and respect themselves and others. It is not necessarily easy for teachers to function in this nurturing mode where students are given constant attention and encouragement. Often their working reality is one of overcrowded classrooms, with children exhibiting all kinds of disruptive behaviour.

Additionally, the teachers themselves, like all other normal adults, are saddled with their own emotional 'baggage', in the form of their unresolved emotional issues. It is this 'baggage' which will tend to manifest itself as inappropriate reactions to classroom situations. It is quite a challenge for the teacher to see the student as separate and distinct from his/her disruptive behaviour.

Implications for Curriculum Development

Traditionally, the curriculum has been perceived as the elements of the course content of the particular academic subject being taught. It appears, however, that increasingly, it is being recognized that everything that is relevant to classroom dynamics can be a legitimate concern for the curriculum.

This development is fortunate because it is important that the elements or attributes cited for the moulding of socially and emotionally well-adjusted young persons be made explicit in school curricula irrespective of the academic subject matter being taught. Values education should be made an important content component of curricula in primary and secondary schools.

Activities such as the Peace and Love in Schools (PALS) programme, spearheaded in Jamaica, could be evaluated to identify what generic elements can be adopted in curricula throughout the region.

In addition, an initiative such as the Health and Family Life Education programme that has been endorsed by Ministries of Education throughout the English-speaking Caribbean could be very useful in communicating important values to young persons. If, however, we were to rely primarily on the course content of material to be imparted to students in primary and secondary schools throughout the region to promote social cohesion and a culture of nonviolence among the youth, we would be missing the mark.

What is of even greater importance in the socialization of these students during classroom hours is the quality of the teacher/student interaction, independent of subject matter being taught.

Whether they are teaching mathematics or social studies, teachers in primary and secondary schools of the region will find that, when they adopt an approach which aims to nurture and encourage students, not only will they contribute effectively to producing emotionally healthy young adults, but management of their classrooms will become considerably less problematic.

There are many conscientious and dedicated teachers throughout schools in the Caribbean, but their ability to create, on an ongoing basis in their classrooms, a nurturing, valuing environment will very much depend on their own early socialization and how successful they have been in releasing emotional hurts encountered in their early youth. It will be recalled that culture was defined simply as usual or normative ways of being, doing and relating.

It is clear that, for the objectives being sought, the entire culture of the classroom has to be one in which students are encouraged to believe in and develop their abilities. The Changing the Culture of the Classroom programme, which has been led by UNESCO/CARNEID, has been eloquently described by Colleen Winter-Brathwaite in EFA in the Caribbean: assessment 2000. However, some additional remarks seem relevant in the current context.

In a Changing the Culture of the Classroom training workshop that was conducted with teachers from a junior secondary school in Trinidad and Tobago, the teachers reacted with great surprise when that there are no problem students. One teacher interjected 'If there are no problem students, you have to be implying that there are problem teachers.'

The basic point that was being established is that the student must be seen as a distinct entity, not to be identified with his/her behaviour, however inappropriate that behaviour might be. When the student is seen by the teacher as separate from the behaviour it is then possible for the student to be helped by that teacher. In these experiential training workshops, the teachers learn specific skills for classroom management.

At the same time, they explore themes such as: early distress experiences and the natural recovery process; the essence of the role of the teacher; the concept of flexible intelligence; internalized oppression and its impact on behaviour; limited categories of new adult hurt; the concept of restimulation of early distress experiences; acknowledgement and appreciation of student efforts as a nurturing tool; appropriate and inappropriate sanctions; use and misuse of the syllabus; the undesirable use of fear as a control mechanism; the challenge of maintaining discipline in the classroom; empowerment of the teacher for optimum effectiveness.

The education systems in the region, as well as individual teachers, have to redefine their role. This should essentially be seen as the moulding of socially and emotionally well-adjusted young persons who are equipped with both a well-defined set of personal attributes and a predetermined range of aptitudes and skills. This reorientation of focus away from the short-sighted academic emphasis will more than likely lead in the medium term to societies which are more socially cohesive and in which there is much less violence because young people will emerge from the school system with a healthier self-concept.

This change of emphasis to a more holistic model of education has profound implications both for the development of school curricula, and for teacher orientation and retraining. As much emphasis has to be placed on 'how' things are done in the classroom as on 'what'.

Thus, in the design of curricula as much attention needs to be placed on the strategies for implementing course content as on the course content itself. We have to begin by specifying why social cohesion may be considered to be one of the objectives of education. This, in turn, leads us to identify different approaches to the subject.

Some, descended from the functionalist sociological tradition and starting from a neutral stance towards values, postulate forms of social cohesion which are aimed at sustaining and reproducing a given social order and alleviating conflicts. Others, following a critical tradition with clear libertarian leanings, identify and analyse the forms of social cohesion that appear in a historically determined society and become morally committed to achieving forms of social cohesion that are more just and humane.

It is not a matter of obtaining just any form of social cohesion, but one that produces the best results in terms of liberty, equality and solidarity among the members of society. In the field of education, those theories exerted a powerful influence over the educational policies that were developed in the last century in the countries of the region. In a nutshell, it might be said that the former approach influenced the spiritualist and positivist belief that education systems should be part of the process of constituting and consolidating nation states.

The second approach, on the other hand, was more related to critical education and so-called 'popular education' movements, and has been behind many of the educational reforms developed in recent decades. Although the effect of these reforms on general practices cannot yet be evaluated, it may be observed from their theoretical constructions that their strength resides in the critical aspects of social diagnosis.

On the other hand, that strength is not apparent in terms of a moral commitment, when it comes to proposing forms of social cohesion and effective ways of achieving it. In relation to the critical approach, the criticism of traditional teaching methods has invalidated many of the methods that have proved effective in traditional education.

One example is the reluctance in such approaches to offer practical ethical education, on the assumption that it is enough for the latter to be implicit in scientific training and in educational practice, or their tendency to restrict specific ethical training to the formation of moral judgement. Another example, related to more practical teaching methods, is the negative attitude to storytelling.

These resources of traditional education, which have proved useful in the past for building shared feelings and expressing emotions and values, have been depreciated on the grounds that they are subject to the risk of ideological abuse. Because of these and other drawbacks, eclectic positions have emerged in most of the curriculum reforms in Latin America, with elements being taken from both approaches under different labels, such as humanist, systemic, holistic or integrationist.

An effort was made to recover social criticism and some of the tools of traditional education. The aim has been to direct educational processes towards the achievement of forms of social cohesion which maximize the potential of all the members of the educational community, with particular attention for the potential of the most underprivileged.

Traditional education never pretended to inquire into the nature and dynamic of social and political life; on the contrary, it presents the forms of life as something already given. Its analysis of such forms amounts to mere consideration of technical matters of organization. Value considerations remain external to the system concerned.

For instance, learning about democracy or economic systems in this case means learning about how social life is organized through legislation. It does not matter whether that legislation complies with ethical principles or not. The knowledge acquired must merely ensure that actions correspond to the prescribed rules, without enquiring too much either into the underlying basis of the rules or into the way they are assumed.

Thus, the sphere of practice is reduced to the technical problem of getting to know predetermined rules and abiding by them. As the rules do not need to be 'critically assumed', changes occurring in the legal framework will produce not reactions, but merely adjustments to resolve once again the technical problem of adaptation. Approaches aimed at improvement, on the other hand, should emphasize the ethical principles which support democracy as a form of government and a lifestyle, namely liberty, justice and solidarity.

It entails a critical approach to these principles, which begins in the early stages of education with the recognition that they are needed for social coexistence, moving gradually towards an assimilation of the principles as independently as possible in the higher levels of education.

The effort of subjecting these principles to philosophical criticism of their foundation, scope and application in itself implies an opportunity to learn these contents. In view of the concern for social cohesion in our countries, the principle of justice deserves special mention among contents that need to be learned. This is because social justice is one of the weightiest concerns of our societies.

There can be no real social cohesion in unjust societies. Equal opportunities for accessing knowledge and participating in dialogue should therefore be recognized as necessary conditions for social cohesion. Once this is recognized, it will provide a basis for a feeling of solidarity with the most underprivileged and the starting point for a practice directed towards change.

This objective therefore constitutes the keynote of our proposal and should become the focus of educational processes aimed at achieving greater social cohesion in the countries of the region. Having a knowledge of social processes and organizations also means knowing them as legal organizations based on those ethical principles, i.e. standard setting entities socially and historically established to guarantee a certain social cohesion and to administer conflicts.

The critical approach helps to understand the perfectibility of rules established in relation to given circumstances and subject to stated ethical principles. Right from the early stages of education, students can learn and understand the meaning and scope of such rules. Gradually they can learn to relate to them, by observing them, criticizing them and participating in their construction.

This is why it is also important to impart a sense of the historic awareness of the circumstances in which the rules used to organize social life are constructed and developed. In the present context, for instance, for any analysis of democracies, families or social working relations, it is essential to refer to institutional crises, the search for new models of representation and participation, the nation-state identity crises brought about by globalization, changing methods of production, etc.

If students are able to find some beacons within the uncertainty of change, this will give them a better understanding of the dynamic quality of concepts such as 'democracy', 'family' and 'community'. Hence when learning the modes of organization of social life, it is important not to lose sight of the fact that these forms of organization are 'historically situated'.

Learning Community

With regard to those who are the subjects of education, the central notion that prevails in traditional education is the notion of the individual, through references to individual achievements, individual obligations, individual responsibilities and individual rights. On the other hand, educating for social cohesion makes it necessary to consider the learning subject as a learning community.

Social cohesion implies coexistence; therefore the minimum subject cannot be the individual, as a being aware of standards/norms, but rather the 'cohabitants', i.e. the 'learning community'. This working approach raises the need for educational contents which are relevant for dealing with the challenges facing the countries of our region, namely a sense of belonging and solidarity. The school, in its traditional socializing function, provides a scenario of coexistence that can bring together traditions and communities of different origins. In this scenario, students and teachers undergo the daily experience of building a collective identity that allows for their differences.

The outcome of this experience will then to a great extent determine the future integration of the citizen in the public life of the local, regional or national community. Preparedness for participation and public responsibility does not manifest itself spontaneously on departure from school. It requires a considerable effort of learning which begins when at the very outset of education the subject learns to appreciate the meaning of the word 'us'. It later culminates in the knowledge and appreciation that individual differences and conflicts resulting from those differences are not an obstacle, but are part of the process whereby this collective identity is constructed.

These differences and conflicts can therefore offer opportunities to enrich the collective identity insofar as they are duly treated as a means of learning the ethical principles that are being pursued.

Hence, the importance of changing the way students are considered in our countries, which are faced with the challenges of redefining identities in the context of globalization and of the changing relationships between the state, society and the market.

The socializing function of the school, which was often in the past suspected of complicity with the prevailing ruling systems, must now be recovered, in line with this perspective, as offering the possibility of rebuilding a public awareness in the face of the divisive and individualizing tendencies which prevail under the hegemony of the logic of the marketplace. This also implies a change in the attitude of teachers, who can be active players in constructing this communal, transforming subjectivity, to the extent that they become aware that they too are cohabitants.

Learning for social cohesion therefore requires a 'classroom atmosphere', where the ethical principles that constitute democratic life emerge as ideals governing concrete practices. It requires an opening of the school to the community.

Converting the physical space of schools into an open centre for cultural activities in the community has proved to be an effective means of tackling problems that seriously affect social cohesion, such as juvenile violence and drug addiction. With regard to learning processes, traditional education was centred on a knowledge of the modes of organisation of social life as laid down by the law, without much concern for the ways such laws were assumed.

By contrast, the central notion underlying education for social cohesion is that of praxis, understood more in the sense of acting than as mere technical doing. Praxis is action charged with meaning and values. This also raises the need for a comprehensive consideration of actors.

Traditional education was geared to focus only on the cognitive capacity of students. Today, affective and practical aspects must also be included. It is not a matter only of knowing how a particular community is ordered and what it values, but of knowing whether that order or that set of values can stand up to rational criticism, and of checking whether the reasons put forward to defend it are sufficiently convincing to want to act in accordance with those rules and values, and consequently to act.

For example, in our society we might consider that co-operation is an essential value for social cohesion and that, as such, it is something that our educational system should support.

So ethical training should not only provide the necessary tools to learn that co-operation is socially valuable, but it should also provide an opportunity for the student to analyse critically the reasons why co-operation is said to be good, while at the same time undertaking to ensure that the student wants to and knows how to co-operate effectively.

To put it in simple terms: it is not a matter only of knowing that it is good, but also of knowing why it is good and in addition wanting to do good and knowing how to do it. In this way the school could provide a forum for reflection and action which could help detect and criticize existing values and moral standards.

This in turn would enable students to adopt behaviours and habits consistent with those principles and standards. It would also allow students to develop capacities for judgement and action that conform to the ethical principles. It is generally recognized that confronting problem situations is a very useful teaching tool for training moral judgement.

When such situations involve the modes of organization and related practices, the tool becomes even more useful. Knowledge and dialogue are essential elements, which developed in suitable conditions combine to facilitate cautious decision-making.

A knowledge of codes, procedures, processes and the institutions involved is needed to identify the best solution to problems. Rational dialogue, in which reasons are put forward and well-founded arguments are exchanged, provides the opportunity to arrive at agreements and to settle conflicts peacefully. Whence the importance that both students and teachers should acquire basic abilities for dialogue and discussion and should prefer consensus as an ideal way of resolving conflicts.

Among dialogue and communication strategies, special emphasis should be placed on those aimed at the nonviolent resolution of conflicts. Persuasion, negotiation, mediation and arbitration are commonly used strategies in democratic societies which can and should be learned in schools. The practical approach which is proposed means changing the definition of students as agents in order to consider them as actors.

Agents are people who represent and/or reproduce an external discourse. In the traditional approach, education trains agents to reproduce social, political and economic discourses which are alien to their own interests and realities.

The critical approach proposes instead to train actors, that is, subjects who are able to choose and therefore able to construct their own courses of action and the social and political systems in which they participate.

Such actors, while being part of political, legal and economic systems, are in no way predetermined by them, but thanks to their margin of liberty and to the extent of their possibilities, may become creative transformers of those systems. Another trait to be developed in actors is a strategic capacity for action.

This implies an ability to assess the effectiveness and efficiency of different resources or courses of action in order to attain specific targets. With regard to social cohesion in particular, it is best to be able to experiment with different forms of collaboration, co-operation and association in order to be able to appreciate the various possibilities and limitations of individual and collective actions.

School plays a fundamental role to the extent that it offers students considerable opportunities for internalizing the values and procedures of democratic life by exercising institutional participation, which includes knowing how to participate, to dialogue, to petition and to claim rights, to resolve conflicts, to elect and be elected, to be represented and to represent, to build standards and fulfil obligations, etc.

This enables them to face the complexity of exercising democracy, to understand the dynamic of its processes better and to assess its scope and limitations as a form of social coexistence and political organization.

2

ICT Influence on Education

Knowledge management (KM) strategies can serve as valuable tools for decision makers at all levels of the educational system. The distinctive features of knowledge management, identifying the characteristics of successful KM efforts and exploring the usefulness of KM for making important educational decisions.

In US, the role of information technology (as a component of a KM system) in the implementation of high-stakes accountability for 8th grade students in one particular urban district. Before considering the characteristics of knowledge management, it is important to note the differences between data, information, and knowledge.

A further transformation occurs when human experience is added to information to make value judgments about, and comparisons of, different information. The progression from data to knowledge can be seen both as a temporal process in which data, imported into a system's architecture, aggregates individual facts into summaries and averages that are then presented in an appropriate context.

In an educational setting, this might be a report of student test performance by grade, ethnicity, race, and gender. The addition of deeper contextual information about local school leadership, particular organizational characteristics, or other less quantifiable factors can be combined with mechanistically generated test-score results to describe variance in outcomes that could not be extracted from the more traditional reports.

It is this application of personal knowledge and of well-designed models that differentiates information systems from knowledge systems. KM is a follow-up to information management. The bulk of the literature on good information system design focuses on the technologies and processes used to acquire and manage data.

When describing the breadth of approaches to effective knowledge use, a number of authors describe a range of system functions from data management to knowledge creation and application.

Information management lies somewhere between the two poles of data management and knowledge management. Another way to think about KM is that it is the use or application of information. In districts, the student data system provides the core of such a system.

However, this focus on information systems and tools for aggregation and on KM as the application of information should not imply some type of computer-based system that is somehow imbued with deep contextual knowledge of the organization. This is not just a question of the technologies employed. An important role is played by institutional culture.

For example, a district with a collaborative model of interaction between schools will typically display a far greater capacity to develop robust analyses of school-level processes and needs than a district lacking such a model. The importance of organizational culture in enabling or blocking the use of knowledge. Cultures that support knowledge accumulation and application will be the most effective, efficient organizations.

Organizational structures and processes provide a window into the value a knowledge management system will return to any implementer. A willingness to engage in problem-solving processes and share information with outsiders is an important resource for enabling knowledge management efforts.

In an educational setting, curriculum aids might be thought of as knowledge repositories. For example, the Milwaukee Public Schools Curriculum Design Assistant (CDA) is both a source of documentation—standards, learning goals, etc.—and a repository for instructional plans based on this documentation. These lesson plans can be stored in the system and shared with others electronically to provide a knowledge base for a wider audience.

Examples of this sort in public school education are probably rare, but the Community of Science online database is a data and communication resource that functions well in education research: it links researchers, research intuitions, and funders together.

The purpose of the Community of Science online database is to reduce the barriers for those seeking funding for research, as well as to reduce the difficulty of funders in locating qualified researchers. This objective focuses on the creation of a technological environment that will contribute to the social transformation of an organization. Anderson Consulting used this sort of approach to radically shift norms of information sharing and use among its consulting staff.

In the consulting business, there are traditionally strong norms about keeping personal expertise personal—it represents a large portion of individual competitive advantage. Anderson Consulting wanted to reverse this behavior and reward those who shared information with other consultants within the organization. The company began to make participation in an online, e-mail-based, problem-solving environment mandatory.

Eventually the bar was raised further and pay and promotion were linked to the number, quality, and immediacy of an individual's responses. This approach was draconian, but it was successful in building both a compelling repository of problem-solving information and shifting or overturning a strong norm against sharing information.

This approach models an important tool for accumulating and diffusing successful educational practices. The call for methods of replicating successful programs and school initiatives that beat the odds could be addressed with a system that improves communication within educational systems.

Learning Landscape is an example of one such effort in education. This system was an outgrowth of the Connecticut Academy's NSF-sponsored Statewide Systemic Initiative.

The Connecticut Academy worked together with the consulting firm, KPMG, to develop a data warehouse environment based on the National Center for Education Statistics core data elements. The stated purpose of the chapter was to transform data into knowledge to improve student achievement and teacher quality. A new firm has been established, EdExplore, which has the same KM goals but is much more limited in scope and has implementation costs in line with district resources.

EdExplore remains focused on bringing cutting-edge approaches to data warehousing to the evaluation of student and teacher performance. These different goals are not mutually exclusive. Davenport states that most projects his team studied were focused on one of these goals, but many had features of the other goals interwoven into their projects. In addition, the first three objectives can be seen as constituting a feedback loop.

Repositories must be built. Then, these repositories are only useful if users have efficient access to the knowledge contained in them. Finally, the use of knowledge in an organization will be enhanced by the creation of an environment that supports this use.

This knowledge-friendly environment will, in turn, demand higher levels of sophistication in the knowledge repository, thus closing the loop. The fourth goal—determining the return on investment in knowledge management—is closely related to efforts that attempt to determine the return on investment from spending on early research and development.

Many analysts have struggled with this vexing issue, which remains only partly addressed. There are so many unquantifiable, human elements in a KM system that it may be very difficult to come up with metrics that are generalizable.

There are several problems that must be faced by any educational system that attempts to create a knowledge management system. The first problem is to determine the appropriate level of analysis the system is designed to support. Another is that of differential access to computing power and the technical and analytical skills of the knowledge consumers within the system.

In an educational setting, users representing students, classroom teachers, principals, and district administration should be involved in the design of a system destined to support important instructional and policy-level decision making. It is only by including users at all levels of the knowledge system that designers will have the input necessary to grapple with the problems identified above.

The knowledge management systems provide very little insight into the exact analytical approaches one would use in any particular scenario, since so much depends on the organizational form, sector, or level of analysis.

The discussions in the literature focus instead on families of tools designed for pattern detection and predictive modeling. It is important to bring these together with the experience of those working in the specific domain to identify the important dimensions of knowledge in that field, since we have defined knowledge as the application of information in context.

A crucial feature of educational systems is that they are made up of a number of nested systems or organizations. In analytical terms, this can also be described as levels or units of analysis.

In education, these levels range from the federal level, through the state, district, school, classroom, and student levels. The analytical needs differ from level to level as do the relevant time scales. For example, there are classroom needs for lesson planning and local testing. At the school level, free lunch, state-mandated testing, and other mandated programs are focal points of data-management issues. The requirements are as numerous as the funding sources at each level of the organization.

Analytical needs differ, but are present at every level of the system. A robust knowledge management system must reflect the information and knowledge management needs of all levels.

In particular, data must be gathered at a level of aggregation appropriate to the user with the most fine-grained analytical needs. The most common focus of school information systems is on the school and district-level, produced by a central information technology department.

In the case of school district-level knowledge management systems, one might attempt to implement several KM systems. One could argue that schools are groups of professionals with both process and content knowledge.

One organizational model used to describe reform-based schools—communities of practice—would suggest that they would be more likely to focus on enhancing a knowledge environment. Operating under this model, schools would be less likely to accumulate knowledge for its own sake. They would focus, instead, on sharing knowledge among a group of professionals. This would be consistent with the view that schools are communities of learners. A KM system that supports such behavior would be both a repository of successful practices and a system for conveying positive norms associated with sharing knowledge.

The importance of the level of analysis comes to the forefront of any effort to describe and apply KM principles. For example, district-level functions might include analysis of the quality of the data in the system (this may be in formal terms of validity and/or reliability, as well as of alignment of the metrics in use and the learning or performance standards).

District-level analysis might also focus on the curricula that are in use across the district and assess their relative effectiveness. These district-level functions call for nested hierarchies of approaches to systems design that support collection of the relevant data and aggregation of these data to the appropriate level of analysis.

The identification of distinct levels in an organization with different KM needs is even more vital if one considers the increasing demands technology places on individual units in an organization. The traditional neoclassical economics concept of a linear relationship among the different factors of production fails to adequately explain the returns of knowledge. One moves up within an organization, the number of elements that must be integrated in order to produce a good or service has probably not increased dramatically in recent years.

However, the pace at which new technologies and needs are introduced and old technologies become obsolete has increased dramatically. This rapid pace of change in the factors of production places a premium on the ability of individuals within an organization to track change and respond to it. This ability is one of the key features of successful KM.

Unfortunately, this is an area in which traditional information management systems. Data warehouse systems are excellent tools for making complex selections of data from many different sources. However, there are no good inferential or predictive models in place within commercial school decision support systems for modeling school or student behavior in real time. This is not because there is not a rich understanding of student achievement.

Rather, the cost and complexity of real-time KM systems represent a major obstacle to schools or districts taking advantage of this technology.

Schools have lagged behind industry in replacing paper-based clerical and business functions (often referred to as back office functions) with technology-based systems. They often lack the physical infrastructure necessary for communication between numerous geographically dispersed buildings.

The rise of ubiquitous computing, which places relatively inexpensive devices for information storage and manipulation on every desk, has made the conversion to technology-based systems possible. This trend is now finding its way into schools as they move away from using computers for rote learning to employ them as information tools. This is not simply a centralization-decentralization issue—i.e., the spread of technology from the district to the school and classroom. These resources can serve additional goals outside of instruction.

A personal computer is both an information-gathering and an information-manipulation tool. The availability of computing at all levels of the educational system can be a focal point of change. There are certainly budget, security, and management implications in broadening access to sophisticated computing technologies.

However, the need for information transcends district governance issues. Moves toward greater local autonomy and responsibility—whether in response to school vouchers, charter initiatives, or other pressures—mean that there will be an increasing need for local analytical capacity. The need for well-informed local decision-making at the classroom level is not unique to any particular organizational form, however, such as block scheduling, or multi-age classrooms. It exists in both flat and hierarchical organizations.

The level at which decisions are made may differ across organization types, but there must still be robust data-collection and knowledge-dissemination mechanisms at all levels. This is particularly important given the different uses of individual data elements at different levels of aggregation and at different levels of the organization.

Even at the school level, one can demonstrate the utility of comparing groups such as students who are bussed versus not bussed, or students participating in a specific after-school program versus students who do not. Traditional aggregations of data in such instances prove inadequate. The problems outlined above suggest several possible avenues of system design that would lead to more appropriate data structures and produce more useful knowledge in an education knowledge management setting.

The focus on student learning, and the persistent gaps in student achievement described above, should suggest to system designers that knowledge management systems should be student focused. What this means is that individual student data must comprise the basic building block of any knowledge management system in education. This includes data about the students themselves (test scores, demographics, attendance, etc.), as well as data about treatments or interventions intended to influence student outcomes.

So, for example, professional development efforts aimed at improving the teaching of reading comprehension would need to be tracked, since these should have an impact on student learning.

This implies that the school or instructor should collect the data locally and that the data should be used locally to inform teaching and targeted intervention programs. This is an important point that is often overlooked. The most basic common unit of analysis (sometimes referred to as an atomistic unit) should drive data-collection efforts and processes. If the student is the smallest analytical entity that will be studied, then attributes of that entity should be collected.

In schools, this means that data should be gathered at the source. If schools and classrooms are where learning is produced, then local teachers and administrators need to collect and understand the data that will be used to measure that learning.

At the same time, however, districts need to integrate increasing demands for accountability, both fiscal and educational. Increasing scrutiny at the district level implies an entirely different focus for information system design. In this district accountability model, data are aggregated up to higher levels, such as the school or program, and are used to justify administrative or managerial decisions that affect large numbers of students and schools. This does not simply mean a reliance on central capacity.

Knowledge management should be responsive to needs at all levels of the system. The problem is that the events and outcomes being monitored all tend to occur at the lowest levels of aggregation—the student. Even in the most centralized system, instructional outcomes occur at the individual level.

However, most district accountability measures and goals are aggregated to higher levels of the organization. Data on student and teacher absence, student program participation, teacher professional development activities and test scores need to be available at the lowest level for aggregation to any meaningful unit—classroom, grade, neighborhood, or other coherent grouping. This means that only individual-level data will serve. This is important because reform efforts must work on multiple levels. It is also vital that the system be transparent in order to combat efforts to cheat or otherwise tamper with the data.

Data collected at the student or classroom level need to be aggregated and fed upwards to higher levels of the educational accountability structure to inform system decisions made at those levels.

A system without proper security in place could be subject to manipulation by school-level actors. Again, this is not an argument for or against centralization, per se. Rather, one must recognize that there are knowledge management decisions that are appropriate and possible at each level of an organization. Data structures and analytical tools should reflect this reality. This divergence between existing data systems and data needs points to a gap between new technological capabilities and the policy environment that would enable schools to actively collect relevant information and put it to use in a KM system.

When the model of change targets student learning, it is essential to focus on identifying those innovations (technical and organizational) that best serve schools and classroom teachers. Most existing models of school governance do not provide for data analysis at the classroom level. Often there is also a gap between technical capacity and technical feasibility. Most educational systems have very little technical capacity.

For example, teachers may not have easy access to the Internet, or district computer staff may not have much experience supporting the analysis of problems relevant at the classroom level. There must be collection and delivery systems in place.

There must also be analytical support for complex problems that are not solved by looking at simple bivariate comparisons. Making instructional decisions in an individual classroom requires a sophisticated understanding of student attributes and of what individual curricular units can provide. The ability to generalize to a larger population is not a relevant concern in this context.

At the school level, however, a principal may be very interested in how a new professional development activity is affecting student performance relative to other classes in the same building, or in comparison to other schools across the district that did or did not participate in the same training. The tools and data needed for within-classroom analysis are quite different from those necessary for a cross-school comparison.

Differing forms of organizational analysis call for diverse forms of KM system implementation. One faces similar challenges at any level of aggregation, from the classroom through the district level to the federal level. The lack of reliable data for school and student evaluation continues to be a vexing problem. Without a solid analytical model and the appropriate KM infrastructure to collect and aggregate the data, no district of any size would be able to implement a robust evaluation system.

For example, many districts embrace an assessment policy that focuses on individual grade cohorts. This has led to the construction of information systems and testing plans that do not support longitudinal analysis of individual students. However, a system that allowed for accurate and fair evaluation at all levels of the educational system would differ radically from the current model that separates data use and evaluation (occurring at the state and district level) from the people who actually do the teaching and learning (schools, teachers, and students).

Differing organizational approaches to knowledge management are one of the most broadly discussed areas in the field. Much of the recent literature that seems to be relevant for KM is based on the study of complex commercial organizations—primarily large, multinational, financial, and high technology firms—and comes out of the major business schools in the United States and Europe.

The contributions of research on knowledge management to school and district can be applied most directly to strategic planning efforts. The Schools Interoperability Framework, and the National Center for Education Statistics all provide assistance in applying KM principles to planning and evaluation. The organizational reform efforts can often best be described by the way in which they operationalize their KM strategies.

There are four important dimensions of such strategies. New realities can be conceived of as both creating new services or goods and creating relationships with new customers. In this example, Organization A is an organisation that sees innovation in information technology as a way to reduce risks and costs.

A school district following this strategy might implement a new in-school, computer-adaptive mathematics assessment to reduce outside testing costs and to help minimize instructional time lost to testing. Such a system might also help address the problem of mobile students who may not be included in once-a-year standard assessments.

Such an assessment would be an element of a comprehensive program to reduce the risk of litigation associated with differential outcomes between poor and non-poor students by providing the opportunity to test adaptively and at smaller time intervals. Organization B, on the other hand, perceives the value of improvements in information management as coming from adding value or enhancing existing interactions and creating new information services and products.

A school following this strategy might invest in workgroup computers and a high-speed Internet connection. This technology would be used to support teaching a chemistry class in a virtual, web-based environment that would allow for the interaction of commercial and university subject-area experts as outside advisors and mentors for student projects.

An effective organization with a well-designed information management plan will have a clear understanding of its place on these dimensions and will plan for its development needs accordingly. It seems clear that an organization with a mature understanding of the importance of information for decision-making might map its strategy as a circular structure, Organization.

However, the costs involved in moving a complex organization along multiple axes simultaneously would almost certainly be prohibitive. It is important to recognize the tradeoffs between adding to and protecting what already exists. Another dimension not explicitly captured in this graphic.

The immediacy and relative clarity of an organization's current operational needs tend to drive most KM investment strategies. This is no less true for school districts. Any district will have a working payroll or bookkeeping system. There is no other alternative. These systems must be operational and deliver substantial value. Investments in long-term payoffs, such as those often encountered in improving educational systems, typically suffer by comparison.

A system for tracking curriculum development and delivery is typically not characterized by a sense of urgency. The rationale for building such a system is less clear-cut than for the other, more traditional, operational data systems.

Operational systems track and manage day-to-day transactions but are of little use for planning or evaluation purposes. However, as is the case with basic research in the manufacturing sectors, there needs to be substantial investment in a knowledge management infrastructure for any organization to reap long-term payoffs.

The return on investment from knowledge is small in the short term but can have a huge impact in the long run. The dimensional framework to schools and asks how information creates value in an educational setting, the level of analysis becomes extremely important. For example, one focus of a school district, because it performs the business functions of any large organisation system, would be on managing risks and reducing costs.

District administrators would also be interested in producing increased learning, but they could only have an impact through indirect effects. One model of district action would be an active structuring of incentives and resources to create an environment in schools and classrooms that enhances learning.

Bureaucratic structures are good at routine tasks and can provide infrastructure at a reasonable cost by taking advantage of economies of scale. Individual teachers, on the other hand, are engaged in directly adding value to the educational process and creating new realities for their students.

Curriculum support staff might be heavily focused on creating new realities by aligning district curricular resources with new standards or goals. This might include a training on demand streamed video system for delivering professional development when and where it suits individual teachers and coordinators. Using technology to overcome the boundaries of time and space can create many new opportunities.

A legal services team might be focused on reducing risk: for example, a district might put all Individualized Educational Plans (IEPs) online with a system for tracking interventions and student performance. This might be one response to concerns that special education students are receiving uneven access to services. This system could provide both a tool for demonstrating compliance and encouraging school staff to stay on top of student needs by making school-level activities more transparent.

This drastic over-simplification highlights the difficulties one encounters when trying to design a system that meets the needs of actors at multiple levels in the educational setting. It should be made clear that it is not necessary to build one monolithic knowledge management system.

Indeed, it would be extremely difficult to build a complex system that would be adaptable enough to respond consistently to a changing educational policy environment. A resource that has been developed in this regard is the Schools Interoperability Framework, which is an important acknowledgement of the heterogeneity of data-acquisition and knowledge- management systems in use today.

Any realistic district information system must be made up of a matrix of interlocking systems that serve different functions and different user communities. School districts are not unique in their spotty reliance on information technologies designed to enable and monitor reform efforts.

Many district-level systems were created to comply with externally imposed reporting requirements. Unfortunately, investment in transformative types of information technology—technologies that will impact the underlying organizational goals and drastically expand capabilities—is inherently risky. In a recent study of large information technology. Innovation in knowledge management is difficult in a complex organization. In education, we have long experience with the problem of differentiating direct and secondary effects.

The expectation is that improvements in the educational setting—investments in class size reduction, teacher training, access to computers, etc.—will translate into improved learning on the part of the students. Schools and districts often engage in professional development efforts with the intent of improving student performance—an indirect effect of improving instruction.

However, studies of the effectiveness of such efforts are often hampered by the difficulty of isolating and measuring the value added by a particular professional development program to performance at the individual student level. Expectations that simple technology initiatives will adequately address such complex problems are wildly optimistic, at best.

Unrealistic expectations are as likely to be attached to smaller-scale applications of technology as they are to large technology systems. One smaller-scale technological 'fix' that is frequently advocated is the availability of computers in classrooms.

Computers are valuable tools and resources for both teachers and districts. However, what frequently goes unrecognized is that, in order to live up to the expectations and serve the needs of both teachers and district administrators, computers must become an integral part of the classroom environment.

Technology used as just one more add-on activity will have very little educational impact other than perhaps increasing keyboarding skills. There must also be sufficient computing resources in the classroom with links to district-level data systems that allow individual teachers to make meaningful queries in real time. If one believes that frequent measurement is critical for gauging the value added by a particular educational strategy, the ability to record and evaluate data in real time is crucial.

District or state level analysis, on the other hand, would be a centralized, top-down approach that would have little use for complex data structures and would only rely on school-level technology for acquiring data. This distinction in interest between consumers of data at the different organizational levels also reflects the need for a more global understanding of the importance of the timeliness of data collection and rapid turn-around for results that are to aid decision making at the classroom level. The tension between district and classroom needs remains a troublesome barrier with respect to both turn-around time and the expected payoff for the time invested.

Districts need data that are not immediately useful in the classroom (but must be collected there) and classroom teachers routinely assess their students and vary their interventions based on those assessments. Finally, there is a serious question about the validity of the measures of student learning used at both the school and district level.

Teachers often question the alignment of standardized tests with enacted curricula. There are also concerns about the consequential validity of using such tests to make high-stakes decisions about the progress of students and the retention or pay of teachers. By the same token, while a classroom assessment may be valid within that classroom, the reliability of such measures is too low to be useful for comparing student progress within a school or across a district. This is a problem that technological innovations can address, but not in purely technical terms. The design of new assessment instruments may be enabled by new delivery and recording technologies.

The rapid growth of computer-adaptive testing and its immediate scoring and reporting of results represent an enormous change from the typical 'fill in the bubble' examinations. Wide access to digital video has made the production of multimedia portfolios of student work a reality in many non-affluent schools. This is an area where the landscape is changing rapidly.

As distance technologies improve to allow teachers to collaborate with subject-area experts, master teachers, test constructors, and others, it will become easier to work together on test quality and comparability.

The social organization of classroom support structures will need to change as well, but the hope for coordination at a higher conceptual level can be realized. There has been a great deal written about new forms of technical infrastructure and about the role that enabling technologies play in knowledge management. Schools often have very little in the way of technological infrastructure on site.

However, the current thinking about successful knowledge management warns against relying on technology to solve the whole data management problem.

The importance of core technological capabilities is a myth developed by managers looking for stability in rapidly changing environments.

However, it is essential that the importance of the level-of-analysis problem in this area be recognized as well. Information networks that link the different levels of educational innovation will encounter greater challenges to building interest and enthusiasm for knowledge if that knowledge is of little use at a particular level in the organization—especially if it is the level that must shoulder the greatest burden for data collection (i.e., the classroom). Likewise, there are difficulties in agreeing on data structures and analytical models when purposes differ.

The data structures, analytical frameworks, and technological infrastructure necessary to answer questions in one area or level may have little relevance in another area or level. The importance of organizational culture for supporting knowledge management activities. It is also important to consider the involvement of critical users in the creations of a KM system. The imperatives for successful implementation of information technology-based innovation from a different direction. They argue that users of a technology must be the focus of any development or change effort, not its target.

For example, a centralised, system for student attendance might provide detailed output that is designed by a district staffer to satisfy a state reporting requirement. Local schools, however, might have multiple additional needs. This is often the case when technology is developed by a central bureaucracy to serve its own KM needs. A KM system for student assessment will look very different if a district office designs it for its own use from the way it would look if it had been designed by groups of classroom teachers to support instruction.

Traditional approaches to system development are too linear to adequately address the dynamic, multidimensional nature of successful knowledge management systems. Another important characteristic of successful KM projects is the presence of high-level non-information technology supporters (e.g., managers not in the technology or computer departments).

Since the adoption of KM technology is largely a social process, it is vital that senior operational managers support the project and show that they value active participation. These caveats seem to be particularly important for projects that attempt to integrate the needs of multiple levels within an organization.

High-level support that focuses on an overriding need—such as improving student test scores—can be very effective in overcoming traditional barriers to cooperation that are often encountered in bureaucratic organizations.

Needs that can be defined more broadly—that appeal to organization-wide norms or goals—are best articulated from upper levels of management and have the best chance of being widely accepted if they are sponsored by someone with no parochial interest in one system or another. Others have addressed the problem of integrating human and technical systems. Technology is important for efficient transfer of vital knowledge, but delivers its benefits only as it supports human communication and knowledge construction.

For example, large data warehouses and data mining tools typically yield low-value knowledge, while a low-tech help desk delivers high-value knowledge. This is the difference between looking at pages of tabular data on the one hand and statistical analysis and advice from an expert on the other. The expert brings personal experience, context sensitivity, and technical skill and combines it with the data at hand to produce integrated knowledge as an output. The important point of this example is that the expert interprets information—data that has been systematized. It is the aggregation of information and expertise that produces knowledge.

The low-tech/high-tech split reflects the fact that tacit knowledge is best shared through people; explicit knowledge can be shared through machines. Or, the more tacit the knowledge, the less high-tech the solution. District-level information systems often contain a great deal of explicit knowledge about students and schools. Tacit knowledge is that uncodified knowledge that is based on personal experience, absorption of organizational norms, and other factors.

Explicit knowledge is information that has been written down or recorded in an information system. This might seem like a simplistic distinction, but it has important implications for decision-making and the reform process. This does not mean that the accumulation and transmission of tacit knowledge is not possible. Rather, it means that knowledge management systems must have imbedded in them some portion of the critical tacit knowledge needed to interpret information in the system at hand.

For instructional decisions, teachers and school-level administrators, for example, often operate on the basis of tacit knowledge about an individual student or group of students. These data are much more difficult to aggregate and transfer. The primary problem is not technical. Rather, it is the difficulty of developing relevant metrics for a wealth of anecdotal data.

Another important example of the importance of tacit knowledge is the practice of using individuals as the focal point of reform efforts. School districts often use successful principals and other administrators as agents of change. Administrators that have been able to turn a school around are seen as a valuable commodity.

The literature on KM refers to this process as one of using mobile intellectual capital to bring expert skill to bear on a particular local problem. The value of intellectual capital is often the tacit knowledge about how one manages curricular changes or fosters a positive school climate.

This process of conveying tacit knowledge about such a complex task is one example of a knowledge system. The drawback is that tacit data is not easily transferred and successes at one location are not easily replicable to another. Some KM system-designers attempt to imbed the interpretation of experts in the outputs of the system; for example, one might present a bar graph of mean scores on a particular set of assessments.

A more knowledge-rich presentation might include a representation of error bands around the mean, or provide a comparison to scores of the same students in a prior assessment. It is not merely that the information presented should be contextualised. It is important that the contextualization be done in a way that makes a valid comparison and enhances the explanatory power of the measure in question.

There are distinctions along the continuum from data to knowledge. The data structures in this case must be available at the individual level and be sufficiently broad for meaningful diagnostic use.

Making the linkages clear between different levels of the organization and building methods of capturing and using tacit knowledge are two characteristics that must remain in the forefront of any design effort.

The initial area of collaboration will be in the area of intra-application communication. The model the SIF group is supporting is an open-system environment. This approach recognizes that schools and districts will continue to use a mix of information technologies from various vendors. The SIF initiative is focused on setting data exchange standards that will let the major school management and instructional support packages talk to each other without human mediation.

The challenge the SIF has set for itself is based on the efforts of the business information technology community to move from data-management to knowledge-management systems. While the issues involved in successful knowledge management are largely absent in the literature on educational administration and assessment, an important and growing body of work is emerging from business schools around the world. These works range from thinking about the role of experts in organizational learning to multi-dimensional representations of the lifecycle of knowledge.

Unlike a product created by a particular vendor, district-level, state-level, and federal education administrators developed this model. Rather than being market-driven, the NCES Forum on Educational Statistics focused on the decision-making needs of school- and district-level administrators. This focus on users of data turns the traditional approach on its head.

Most major school software systems—such as the offerings for National Computer Systems (NCS)—are driven by a lowest-common-denominator approach, where the package provides for the minimum needs for the maximum number of possible users.

The NCES data elements, on the other hand, are developed to a high level of specificity and are intended to be extremely flexible and encompass the widest possible use. Both of these efforts point toward the importance of standardized acquisition and the use of data for day-to-day and long-range decision making. The issue of standardisation is particularly important when the focus is on evaluation. Increasing demands by outside funders and state and local agencies for data on program impact continue to raise the analytical burden placed on the district.

In traditional transactional student data systems, the focus is on managing schedules and tracking attendance and grades. Reporting is designed using a top-down approach that is focused on district, state, and federal reporting requirements. What the NCES proposes is a much more flexible design that would support very fine-grained inquiry from any level of the organization. Knowledge management is such a wide-open area of study that it is difficult to understand the implications of these models of knowledge management for an educational setting. One thing seems certain. School information systems are one of the most difficult to harness because they often lack any overall rationality for cooperation and compliance.

Differences in data needs and uses across different organizational levels present significant barriers to the collaboration necessary for innovation in knowledge management. The Data Warehouse is also several years behind schedule. There remain two major stumbling blocks to the development and use of the system.

The first hurdle is the difficulty of producing assessment, enrollment, and program participation statistics that match those created by the existing combination of mainframe exports, SAS (statistical software) scripting, and hand manipulation used to produce the district's accountability reports.

This problem can be traced back to the inherent complexity of the analytical puzzle of tracking a highly mobile population of students with an archaic information system that relies on a great deal of expert knowledge on the part of its users. This is simply a high-dimensional analytical problem that cannot be easily moved from one system to another. The other problem is that the new data system uses different data element definitions, field layouts, and formats. The new system is designed to take into consideration the improvements in methodology and changes in how one defines important school metrics such as value-added assessment and program effectiveness. Any comparison of analytical models between the two methods of producing accountability statistics requires the ability to engage in a sophisticated translation among approaches that are vastly different.

The other stumbling block the Data Warehouse faces is the method of access that school administrators and teachers will use to extract data for local analysis. The tool that was initially adopted is being used by district-level analysts in the Department of Technology Services and the Office of Research and Assessment, but was seen as too complicated for the average or casual user. Other solutions that rely on Web-based access are either not supported by the some of the desktop technologies in place, do not meet the security requirements the district must meet to protect student data, or are as complex as the tool the district is currently using.

Finally, the lack of strategic planning and strategic resource allocation continues to plague development efforts at the district level. It is possible to raise funds to support the infrastructure in providing high-speed video to several thousand classrooms, but it is difficult to find the resources to train the staff to use video effectively, or to build an evaluation system to track the impact of this technology on teaching and learning.

Doctrine of Fair Use

The Doctrine of Fair Use exempts certain categories of activity in some instances from the legal obligation to obtain permission from the author of a work before copying, performing, or displaying that work. Potentially exempt activities include teaching, research, scholarship, reporting, commentary, and even parody. The justification for the Fair Use exemption derives from the court's view that sometimes free and open discourse about ideas can be more of a stimulant to creation of new knowledge and new creative works than protection of the author's ability to reap financial reward from his work. Traditionally the use of excerpts from copyrighted materials for classroom teaching has been conceived as a Fair Use.

In 1976 the U.S. Congress formally adopted the Doctrine of Fair Use into its revision of the Copyright Act. That was twenty-five years ago. Since then technologies for reproducing, copying and displaying copyrighted materials have changed dramatically, and the locus for teaching activities has expanded beyond the classroom to include the airwaves (as in educational TV) and now the Internet.

These changes have affected authors', teachers', and publishers' perspectives about is "fair" and what is not "fair." Today as the educational community moves rapidly towards web-based education and a growing emphasis on distance learning, we believe it is important to take a another look at Fair Use and its relationship to evolving instructional technologies, if only to protect schools, teachers, and course developers from unexpected legal challenges. First, however, to understand Fair Use and its application to education, one must give up any idea that "fair use" was ever really about equity. It's not. Like copyright itself, the doctrine derives ultimately from Western concepts of individualism and principles of market- based capitalism.

The identification of what is "fair" or "not fair" is deeply entwined with the nature and ownership of the technologies used to reproduce or distribute the works in question as well as to who stands to gain or loose from a particular type of use. The basis for copyright is established by Article 1, Section 8.h of the United States Constitution, which states:

"The Congress shall have power to promote the progress of science and useful arts by securing for limited times to authors and inventors the exclusive right to their respective writings and discoveries."

Copyright (along with patent, trade secret, and trademark) is the tool that implements the Constitutional purpose. Copyright is a legally enforceable intellectual property right that protects a financial incentive designed to encourage individuals to take the risk of creating new works or improving on previous ones.

The productivity and innovation that lie at the heart of US economic success seems to provide clear testimony for the wisdom of the framers of the Constitution. Before the Copyright Revision Act of 1976, the record of cases involving Fair Use of copyrighted material in the classroom is sparse.

What exists draws on the general principle that copying for classroom use without obtaining permission from the author was not an infringement of copyright as long as there was no impact on the sale of published books or sheet music. There were only two cases concerning classroom copying by instructors before 1976. Both addressed the question of what portion of a copyrighted work could be freely copied and distributed to students under the Doctrine of Fair Use.

Macmillan argued this was an infringement of copyright and negatively impacted their market. Although most students did purchase the classroom text, some did not, apparently relying solely on their tutor's materials. The court ruled against the tutor. In the next case, Withol v. Crow 309 F.2d. 778th Cir. 1962, fifty years later, the court similarly ruled against a music teacher, who, short by forty-eight copies of a musical score for his students, decided to make copies rather than purchase additional scores from the publisher. These two cases represent essentially all of the case law defining the application of Fair Use to teaching activities until the 1976 Copyright Revision Act.

Clearly it did seem at that point that if a teacher stayed safely below some upper limit of copying an entire work, then the teacher would not risk a complaint that her activity was not Fair Use. After 1976, however, Fair Use became more complicated for teachers.

Even as the Congressional revision generally identified copying for educational purposes a potentially Fair Use, it laid a foundation for confusion by setting forth criteria to use in the determination of whether or not a specific instance of copying was actually a Fair Use. Section 107 specifically states that making multiple copies of copyrighted materials for use in a classroom is not in itself an infringement of copyright.

It then defines four factors that are to be used to analyze any specific situation—and so enters uncertainty: In determining whether the use made of a work in any particular case is a fair use the factors to be considered shall include:

i) the purpose and character of the use, including whether such use is of a commercial nature or is for nonprofit education purposes;

ii) the nature of the copyrighted work;

iii) the amount and substantiality of the portion used in relation to the copyrighted work as a whole; and the effect of the use upon the potential market for or value of the copyrighted work.

iv) In interpreting this section, the courts thus far have generally viewed the forth factor, potential market impact, as the most important factor, given that the commercial and financial monopoly is at the heart of the concept of copyright. However, the use of the word "includes" rather than "are" in this section opens the door to a suggestion that there could be other factors, perhaps more important, influencing the interpretation of a particular situation.

Section 110, establishes that Fair Use may apply to performance or display of copyrighted works during "face-to-face teaching activities" that are "a regular part of the systematic instructional activities of a government body or a nonprofit educational institution."

The language here seems to focus on making a careful distinction between what might be construed as Fair Use for educational purposes and some other use that might be construed as either "entertainment" or a commercially motivated performance or display. The limitation of non-infringing performances to only those used in "face-to-face teaching activities" and the introduction of the vague concept that the non-infringing performance must be "integrated into a systematic course of instruction" further increase the complexity of applying this doctrine in the contemporary educational environment where digital instructional technologies allow teachers to download audio, video, graphics, text, photography, and radio and TV-like "webcasts" and "display" them to students inside or outside the traditional classroom via a class website.

The Congressional Record reveals that there was some real disagreement between those stakeholders interested in maintaining copyright free from any significant educational entitlements and the academic community which views Fair Use for education purposes as an historic privilege. Educators on the committee also argued that teachers should be excused from obtaining permissions because the very process of obtaining and paying royalties to use materials would be an onerous duty and an inhibitor of academic freedom.

Indeed, the guidelines are very conservative and are increasingly difficult to apply in practice. Part of the reason they sound so silly today is that in being so specific they have simply not kept pace with changes in copying technologies (photocopying and computers). The guidelines set a very constrained standard for what may be construed as a "Fair Use" in an educational setting and may appear to contradict a more expansive interpretation of the language in the statute itself.

For example, the guidelines define "brevity" as not more than 250 words of poetry, or 2500 words or less from a complete article, short story or essay, or 1000 words or 10 percent (whichever is less) from any prose work.

Copies of these brief excepts are non-infringing only if they are also "spontaneous" (i.e., according to the guidelines, a last-minute inspiration of the teacher) and one-time. According to authors of the guidelines, the basis for an exemption for such spontaneous one-time use of copyrighted works was simply to allow teachers enough time to obtain permission for the next classroom use (a process that in the mid-1970s took from four to eight weeks).

Lost is the court's concept in the original doctrine of Fair Use that there was general social benefit in open discourse which itself was an encouragement of new ideas and innovation.

The guidelines make clear that any post-class distributions of teaching materials to an interested but non-registered student could never be construed as Fair Use.

The danger of teachers seriously impacting revenues from the sale of books and periodicals by making copies on the departmental mimeograph machines probably seemed fairly remote even to the teachers themselves. Indeed, in practice many teachers may have felt the constraints of the guidelines tight but livable given the situation. The American Association of University Professors and the Association of Law Schools joined in arguing that the guidelines failed to take into account the reality of how teachers actually used materials for teaching purposes. They argued, more to the point, To protect themselves, many Universities today still disseminate the 1976 guidelines to their faculties, probably with tongue deeply embedded in cheek. The photocopy revolution came in after 1976.

With it libraries and instructors had a means to quickly, easily, and cheaply reproduce quantities of materials for research and teaching. Instead of gathering books and journals onto the shelves of the reserved book room where students lined up to read assignments from the one or two available copies, libraries and instructors could just hit the "number of copies" button on a big machine and in minutes have copies for even the largest class.

The old departmental mimeograph machine went to salvage and a typical student excuse for not doing the reading disappeared. Instructors also felt themselves freer to pick and choose reading material for their students without being bound by selections in someone else's textbook.

Commercial copy centers sprang up around campuses, reserve reading rooms dimmed their lights, and the "coursepack" was born. Meanwhile publishers and authors saw the photocopy machine as creating a whole new market for the sale of rights to reprint portions of books and articles from journals.

Two cases established the rules for determining Fair Use in this new technical environment. The first was Basic Books v. Kinko's 758 F. Supp. 1522. In this case the publisher, Basic Books, challenged Kinko's failure to obtain permission from the copyright holders (usually the publishers) when reproducing coursepacks. Although Kinko's argued that permission was not needed because the coursepacks were for classroom use and hence were exempt under Fair Use, the court agreed with Basic Books. Kinko's had unfortunately attracted the attention of the publishing world by advertising its ability to produce quick turn around of copies because it did not have to take the time to obtain permission from publishers.

An analysis of the Kinko's case emphasizes the commercial nature of copyright law and demonstrates how the Doctrine of Fair Use may be modified when a new technology creates opportunities for business. The court held that Kinko's failure to obtain permission had negatively impacted the market in permission or licensing fees. Kinko's had "extinguished" a financial reward to the copyright holder (the publisher), which was precisely the reward that copyright was designed to protect. Today most copy shops rigorously refuse to reproduce coursepacks unless permission to reprint has been granted in writing.

Any permission fees charged by the copyright owner are then passed on to the students. The key to understanding the Kinko's case is to see that the court did not really address the Doctrine of Fair Use as it applies to actions by instructors and students. Instead, with typical narrowness, the court focused the discussion entirely on the two businesses in the middle of that educational relationship.

Since the copy shop had a commercial interest in the coursepack, the copy shop could not view its own reproduction as "Fair Use," despite the end use of its product for classroom teaching purposes. The principle laid down in Basic Books v. Kinko's was repeated, clarified, and perhaps strengthened in a second case on the same issue: Princeton University Press v. Michigan Document Services 99F.3d. 1381. In this case, Michigan Document was one among several copy shops operating near campus. Its owner deliberately set out to test the ruling in the 1991 Basic Books case.

Michigan Document therefore, not only did not obtain permission to reproduce materials for coursepacks, but also advertised this action, passed the savings incurred on to students, and used this reduction in price to undercut competitors. It is not surprising Michigan Document drew the attention of the publishers, and a negative ruling from the court. The court reaffirmed that if the copier makes money from the copying, then the copying could not be construed to be Fair Use, even though the reproduction had an ultimate educational purpose. The court amplified that the Fair Use exemption is not a blanket exemption and that when litigants have commercial interests, the burden of proof that a copying situation is "fair" lies with the copier—in this case the copy shop.

Since ultimately the copy shop is in the business of commerce, that is in making money not in teaching, the Doctrine of Fair Use does not apply. The court also again noted the existence of a lucrative new market in permissions created by photocopy technology.

Teachers who believe they can "get around" the commercial aspect of the copyshop decisions by making their own copies in the library or on their own office copy machines might do well to take another look at the story of the Harvard tutor back in 1914. The court has never actually tested the legitimacy of the coursepack itself, just of its reproduction by a commercial business. Essentially the coursepack is a unique collection of materials assembled by an instructor for a particular class that may be delivered one or more times.

Components of the "pack" are quite long—whole chapters, articles, essays, or stories—far exceeding the so called safe harbor standards presented in the classroom guidelines. Under the 1976 Act such a collection itself is a copyrightable work, referred to as a "collective work." The digital technology for both desk-top publishing and distance learning, including webcasting, class web-sites, e- learning, and in-class real-time Internet access, is here now here. With it has come a quantum leap in the murkiness of applying the Doctrine of Fair Use for education.

Not only does the approach suggested by the 1976 Act seem outdated, but also Congress's recent effort to update copyright for the computer age—the 1998 Digital Millennium Copyright Act—deliberately sidesteps many of the toughest issues for educators by declaring them simply "unsettled." The first "unsettled"—if not "unsettling"—issue concerns the definition "copy" on the

Internet. According to the Copyright Act, to be a "copy" the reproduced work needs only to be fixed in a tangible medium of expression.

Although the focus of Advanced Computer Services was software, the principle laid down by that decision would seem to be applicable to any work, including articles and Power Point presentations, or video clips, viewed or read via the Internet. If that is so, it raises the spectre of every single viewing of copyrighted materials over the Internet involving either a potential copyright infringement or a royalty payment. This interpretation seems overly restrictive, undercutting the balancing of interests that copyright law attempts to achieve between public and private benefits.

While authors do need protection of their ability to reap benefits both in dollars and reputation, the ultimate goal of copyright—the encouragement and advancement of knowledge and creativity—would not be served by skewing everything in the direction of the author's monopoly of copyright.

Indeed, the court in Religious Technology Center v. Netcom On-Line Communications Services. Inc., 907 F. Supp. 1361 took a more reasonable approach when it characterized what happens when a user browses through materials on the Internet as "the functional equivalent reading"—not copying. Judge Whyte viewed this such reproduction of a file on the computer screen as simply a necessity for humans to perceive the information—rather like stand-up reading in a book store or borrowing a journal from the library. We hope, in the end, that Judge Whyte's reasonable view will prevail.

Anti-copying technology certainly exists to disable a reader's ability to print, attach, or email an article over the Internet—activities that may be closer to a traditional understanding of copying. However, such distinctions are by no means without uncertainty in the evolving legal environment.

Unfortunately, current trends appear to be towards protecting commercial interests rather than protecting the public's access to knowledge or learning. In addition, technology may help resolve the complaint made in the minority report on the classroom guidelines that the task of obtaining permission to use copyrighted materials is onerous and time consuming. This, at any rate, is one possible implication to be derived from the decision in American Geophysical Union v. Texaco, 802 F. Supp. 1. In this case the court ruled against a Texaco researcher who, for his own convenience, regularly made photocopies of articles from journals which he kept in his office for future reference.

Though such copying is common practice among both researchers and teachers, whether working in commercial or noncommercial context, the court accepted the copyright owner's argument that permissions were easy to get because of new Internet-based Copyright Clearinghouse technology and then went on to reason that since the ultimate purpose of the researcher's activity was profit for his employer (Texaco) that the private monopoly interest of the authors should prevail. Somewhere the larger issue that led to the establishment of the Doctrine of Fair Use in the first place seems to have gotten lost in excitement over how easy the new technology can make the payments for copying rights flow. We as a society need to stop a moment and review what earlier courts had to say about the importance of support for the individual teacher or researcher who is exploring ideas and creating knowledge for the next generation and the general benefit of society.

The current use of Internet technology to support teaching brings new commercial players into the communications continuum, separating teacher and student in the so-called distance learning environment.

Impact of Virtual Education

As a human phenomenon, education is not a market for products, but a process of growth and transformation, one sustained over many years with success measured throughout the vicissitudes of personal and collective experience. Indeed, many companies may do well by doing good.

But producers of edutainment have yet to show whether they have either an interest in the human process of education or the capacity to give it intentional shape. Surely the activities of such companies, like those of mass communicators throughout the 20th century, will have significant effects on the cultural context within which educational work takes place.

But the likelihood is slim that the producers of edutainment, as such and single-handedly, will be the prime reshapers of the processes of education. Education is the work of educators, not movie producers, broadcasters, or theme-park operators. Educational institutions--schools, universities, museums, laboratories, libraries--are the major factors in the social construction of a new educational system.

Worldwide they control a huge annual cash flow, derived from individual, governmental, philanthropic, and commercial sources, a cash flow more than sufficient to underwrite far-flung innovation. Furthermore, they control and produce intellectual property of extraordinary breadth and depth.

The holdings of Hollywood are but a pittance compared to those of the world's universities, laboratories, museums, and libraries, and the changes wrought by the digital technologies are making those very holdings more accessible, productive, and meaningful in the lives of everyone.

When people talk about the fruits of intellectual work at its higher levels, they generally think of forms of knowledge spread across an intellectual spectrum that runs from universal scholarship--pure achievements of disinterested reflection--to the domains of professional practice--applied principles of organized performance. Across every field, education included, people need both pure scholarship and professional learning.

An agenda for reconstructing the educational system will touch both the academic and the professional and occupy all the intervening space. Intellectual work involves action of the burdensome sort in which thought guides the effort. If, from the perspective of intellectual institutions, a spectrum running from pure to applied, from academic to professional, characterizes knowledge, then a gradient running from theory to policy to practice generally describes the intellectual and educational uses to which people put that knowledge. Sometimes theory guides work and activity; other times policy controls it; and often patterns of practice shape action. Properly speaking, these are ideal types, like the poles of pure academic knowledge and applied professional learning.

As ideal types they are intellectual formulations applied to the stuff of experience, not empirical actualities substantially involved in it. To make a shift in the spectrum of pedagogical possibility clear, consider the history of architecture in the hundred years from 1850 or so. Until that time, throughout history and across cultures people simply did not build tall buildings except for a few towers for specialized ceremonial and military purposes.

Then a series of innovations occurred, for reasons quite extraneous to the will of architects, that made unprecedented structures feasible. With new materials like structural steel, reinforced concrete, and plate glass, with new techniques for managing water, heat, light, and air, and with novel ways of moving people, these unprecedented structures proved so humanly habitable that specimens of them have been built the world around, with great variations of form and function and with diverse triumphs and failures on all sorts of measures--social, structural, economic, and aesthetic.

The new building technologies did not determine, in a strong sense, how any particular city would look, but they did open a wide new spectrum of architectural possibility. Within the range of this possibility numerous cities have developed imposing skylines like New York's; even Paris, by explicitly adhering to traditional building codes in its central sections, reflects through its conscious restraint one of the possibilities of the new architecture. Digital technologies are for education as iron and steel girders, reinforced concrete, plate glass, elevators, central heating, and air conditioning were for architecture.

Digital technologies set in abeyance significant, long-lasting limits on educational activity. High-speed, wide-area networks linking ubiquitous computers to copious digital libraries transform the cultural conditions under which educational interactions take place.

Traditionally, the school and the classroom have been places where teachers and students are isolated from the general culture and where information and ideas have been relatively scarce -- the textbook is a meager selection of what a field of knowledge comprises, a skilled teacher is a bundle of ignorance relative to the sum of learning, and a school library a sparse collection at best.

Networks reaching through the school into the classroom and to the desktop are ending the isolation and substituting a rule of abundance for that of scarcity. Such a new rule is not without its pitfalls, but to cope with these we must recognize that it is a new rule, deeply different from the old.

In our extended present, the educational problem changes profoundly, shifting from determining strategies for disbursing scarce knowledge to finding ways to enable people to use unlimited access to the resources of our cultures. New media alter the ways of knowing and the opportunities for participating in the creation of knowledge.

Role of Multimedia

Multimedia, and its extension in virtual reality, is not merely a glitzy vehicle for edutainment hype. It is an epistemologically interesting development in our culture. For the most part, the work of thought has seemed to take place primarily through the manipulation of language, with the formal symbolization of mathematics and logic seen as extensions of more everyday linguistic forms. Multimedia make it increasingly evident that the work of thinking can take many forms—verbal, visual, auditory, kinetic, and blends of all and each. Of course, nonlinguistic media are not new, but their status as serious means for creating knowledge is rising considerably.

Knowledge consists primarily of cultural resources that people can store and retrieve on demand, as the need for it arises. Written, especially printed, media long held a privileged place in education because they were easy to store and retrieve to suit the needs of users. Work in other media tended to exist in performances and monuments, which did not suit the strategies of random access. Multimedia changes that condition. It subjects a far wider range of communications to the full rule of random access, changing the repertoire of resources that people can store and retrieve effectively and use on demand to serve the needs of disciplined thought and inquiry.

People can use digital media both to acquire ideas and to express their thoughts in diverse ways. As a result, educators will find it increasingly difficult to favor the linguistic modality over all others, and they will need to broaden the norms of academic excellence. Digital technologies expand personal potentialities. Distributed processing and ubiquitous computing may or may not aggregate into artificial intelligence in the strong sense, creating a species of machines that think in a significant way. But they are clearly coming to function as a means for augmenting our human intellectual skills.

Word processors warn of anomalous spellings as they occur; spreadsheets allow anyone to perform complex calculations quickly and accurately; and databases permit those with good memory or bad to manage information sets that neither could handle on his own. All sorts of more specialized tools greatly lower the skill levels needed to participate effectively in wide ranges of cultural activity.

Precision and exactness may become trivial proficiencies because getting it right will be easy, provided one doesn't get it wildly wrong through some accidental error. With regard to such accidental but sometimes very portentous error, the ability to estimate and guess results, traditionally an educationally suspect knack, becomes an increasingly prized skill.

Thus, educators are sensing that changes in information technologies can deeply transform the hallmarks of having acquired a decent education. Digital libraries, multimedia, and augmented skills change the limits of educational practice. This proposition is not a prediction, but an observation about the potentialities inherent in communications innovations taking place in our extended present.

The basic proposition here is not so much a normative argument that educators should, for one or another reason, accept that these three developments are empowering the transformation of educational activity. Rather, the proposition is more factual, although tentative. As educators experience changing conditions of communication in their work, they understand that these developments are profoundly altering the spectrum of pedagogical possibility.

Individual educators may or may not welcome that condition, but critic and evangelist alike sense that the new conditions open the educational system to significant change. The new conditions, however, do not determine what will emerge. Educators are determining what emerges through the social construction of digital learning communities. Educational structures from kindergarten through graduate schools and adult education are increasingly in flux.

The singular technological feature, which is a turning point for ICTs, is the pre-eminence of the Internet Protocol (IP) for communication, around which ICTs are reorienting and growing. This versatile connectionless protocol is a method by which data is sent over the Internet as packets from one computer to another, each having a unique address. Different packets may be delivered through different routes to their destination, where they are resequenced by the Transmission Control Protocol (TCP) and put back in the right order.

The Wide Area Networks (WAN) which are identified as Internet (international networks), Intranets (corporate or intra-organizational networks) and Extranets (extra-organizational networks) are all IP-based. IP has left its imprint not only on Metropolitan Area Networks (MAN) and Local Area Networks (LAN), but also on equipment such as the network computer, workstation, work group server, media server, Web server, cable TV networks, wireless 'last mile link' to the customer premises, set-top-box and even a kiosk.

Moore's Law has predictably doubled the performance of microprocessors every 18 months and personal computers (PCs) have become increasingly powerful with the introduction of new devices such as cache, more effective architecture and bus interfaces as well as extensive instruction sets.

The introduction of the Slot-1 interface in the second generation of the Intel Pentium family of chips, from the first generation 296-pin Socket-7 interface, made a 242-Contact Slot Access available through a cartridge with a single edge contact. This innovation will ensure a smooth upgrading from one model of the chip to the next without having to change the PC design extensively.

The result is a designer's paradise for minimizing user problems, while upgrading the capacity of PCs frequently to accommodate an ever-growing range of content. The low cost medium speed entry-level Covington allows designers to create a plethora of product lines from a single mother board. Mendocino is increasing the 128K of L-2 Cache on the processor chip at processor speeds. The Celeron chip has the capacity to produce further growth in the content market.

The three leading chip manufacturers, AMD, Cyrix and IDT, are marketing K6, MXi and C6 chips respectively in competition with Intel, and will strengthen their position by early 1999 with the introduction of K7, Jalapeno and C7. By then, Intel will be expanding its processing capacity with Katmai and Merced Chips with a 64-Bit instruction set for the server and workstation markets. Hand-held computing is becoming a useful tool for the collection of data in the field.

Battery-operated receptacles of wireless information, integrated PDA chips like Intel's Strong Arm-1100 running at 200 MHz consuming only 200 milliwatts to power a hand-held PC, 3Com's Palm-III with an infrared receiver and wired modem for connecting to the Web, and Novatel Minstrel's Wireless Modem, which integrates both data and voice communication, are forerunners in this area. Optical Read Only Memory (OROM), with up to 128 MB of storage and no moving parts, provides extra storage in the hand-held PC.

Philips Nino Palm PC which runs pocket versions of Microsoft applications is already available, although the battery power pack at present does not last for more than a few weeks. A close competitor, Windows CE, is gaining momentum. The main problem in home automation is the communication among various devices and appliances.

A possible solution appeared with several technologies using existing home are wiring for telephone, and computer and appliance control utilizing the X-10 Standard module available for most types of appliances. Consumer electronics and PC industry companies have also agreed upon a new consumer electronics bus standard (LE bus), marketed, for instance, by Home Plug and Play, which is an improvement on the X-10 standard followed previously. Software for controlling modules of either of these standards is available.

Ethernet PC network with CE-Bus controllers can be connected to PCs and home entertainment systems. The desk top Sedona offers a versatile tool for content searching which groups file system, Web browser and e-mail client into a single graphic user interface—a trendsetting concept developed by the Intel Architecture Lab (IAL).

Sedona can locate items selectively and find files, e-mail, Web pages or news items of interest without any active input. It can also correlate a message or a document that has been opened with other relevant stored information. New audio standards have been introduced which allow multimedia to provide real-life, 3-D sound for content developers of titles encoded with Dolby digital. This can add depth to sound, almost to the point of immersion.

Multimedia titles can now be encoded with information that creates the illusion of 3-D sound with just headphones or a pair of PC speakers. Direct sound and Direct sound 3-D from Microsoft allows for the mixing of multiple audio streams and programme-surround channels.

As multimedia require larger and larger files, the 1.44 M B capacity of the floppy disk is becoming less appealing and is giving way to three typical competing technologies for removable drive: IOMEGA Zip Drive, Sony-Fujifilm HiFd and LS-120, tending towards the goal of inexpensive 100 MB adequate for multimedia presentation applications, and of course compatible with the existing 3.5 inch floppy disks.

There is a shift from compact disc-read only memory (CD-ROM), towards digital versatile disc read-only memory, version 2 (DVD-ROM-2) drives which can read CD recordable or CD rewritable media. Though better than DVD-ROM-1, at present, they lag behind the fastest CD-ROM drives in overall performance. The sheer enormity of DVD capacity will be useful for storing raw data. It is possible to make feature-length, documentary films using DVD, using high-resolution MPEG-2-standard video compression, immersive Dolby-standard audio compression and extensive 3-D graphics. Everything from high density needs to theatre quality audio and video has become possible.

Compared to the 650 MB peak capacity of CD-ROM, contemporary DVD-ROM media can store nearly 5 G B of data per side, and this quantity will soon attain 1 7 G B. MPEG-2 has now surpassed the quality of laser disks.

An interactive geographic Map Atlas, giving a terrain database of the entire surface of the earth at 1 km intervals with MPEG-2 video, has now become a possibility. In 1998, the software industry reached a turning point: the decisions made will determine the direction to be taken by software architectures of the future.

This trend is accelerated by the convergence of computer, communication and consumer electronics. The once-dominant operating system, such as Windows 3 booted from DOS, will make an exit. Windows NT is now on the verge of addressing the need to support inexpensive computers and a limited range of device support. Microsoft has begun certain development efforts which will make Windows NT usable as a consumer operating system, thereby making Windows.

The year 1998 also saw the beginning of a shift away from professional intermediaries by associating users directly with their software. As a result, users will be required to learn how to express their problems, set up and adapt computations and carry out tasks such as configuration, upgrade, back-up and recovery.

To attain this goal, software system designers have had to redefine user-friendliness. As a result, software carriers like the Web, Integrated Office Suites, Interactive Environment and Visual Basic, which create their own environment from locally available resources, have become popular because they allow users to create or modify software to correspond to their needs.

The setting up of stand-alone processes that can run unmonitored requires an open-ended set of computations - independent processes in mail filters, automatic cheque payment and Daemons, which are sets of software routines and instructions for automating network management tasks. In another move to user-friendliness, sparked by the concept of a hyper-linked design of the World Wide Web, the user interface on personal computers has begun to imitate human perception.

The Graphic User Interface is inventing software products that organize information graphically in more and more intuitively appealing ways. Continuous speech recognition programmes from International Business Machines (IBM), Dragon Systems and others, have started a process whereby speech recognition will be added to the existing programmes like the speech-enabled version of Lotus Notes.

The development of Object-Oriented Data-base Management Systems has accelerated to overshadow the traditional Relational Data Base Management (RDBM) software development.

Object-Oriented databases allow new data types to be created with traditional attributes found in relational models as well as built-in functions, methods and objects which are convenient for applications requiring video and image content. However, the growing popularity of data mining (the 'mining' of numerical data in repositories such as spreadsheets and databases) and data warehousing (the gathering of data from legacy mainframe and PC server databases into gigantic centralized databases) has made it possible to keep RDBMS in use.

The inter-operability of the Distributed Component Object Model (D-COM) and of Java running on Common Object Request Broker Architecture (CORBA) made databases capable of mixing and matching data in an unprecedented manner. These two trends have brought about a hybrid technology that patches object capabilities on to traditional RDBMS products.

Data visualization is a new graphics application which displays in a graphical form the trends that the numbers represent. The evolving Extensible Markup Language (XML) and dynamic Hyper Text Markup Language (HTML) are being integrated to give better graphics on the Web, and new graphics software is +being developed for data mining to bring out anyhidden information.

Virtual Reality (VR) is now regarded as a natural extension of interactive multimedia. New immersive interfaces like Vision Dome and Immersive Work Bench allow several workers to co-operate and interact in conducting simulation experiments on virtual prototypes. With highspeed networks and the World Wide Web, work may be carried out from almost any geographical location.

Architects and furniture wholesalers have already begun using VR on the Web in 3-D by using Virtual Reality Modeling Language (VRML) to give customers a wide selection of simulated prototypes from which to choose. During 1997 and 1998, there was a rush to create World Wide Web-enabled Software that could be used over the Internet, Intranets and Extranets for exchanging data, with a web site to run programmes, control experiments remotely or publish documents on a network.

A significant software-related development has been a shift towards the Web-centred work environment and the electronic distribution of information. One major deficiency of the Web, namely the limitation of HTML in dealing with mathematics, has been reasonably solved.

Instead of the past practice of representing equations as embedded graphics, which proved highly inefficient, an extension of HTML, called Math ML, has been developed. Many new developments have encouraged the electronic publication of journals , some of which have replaced the paper versions.

One of the most significant developments of software applications in 1997 and 1998 saw the rise of the Enterprise Resources Planning (ERP) package, offering a completely new opportunity for organizations to plan their resources around growing customer demand and to offer leading-edge solutions, reduced turnaround time, increased efficiency and improved profit margins.

In 1997 and 1998, the concept of network-based virtual communities, which will redefine the relationship between companies and customers, gained ground.

The emphasis is shifting away from the retailers and is allowing customers to deal directly with wholesalers for the purchase of products and services by capturing and managing information themselves. This is promising to become a beneficial situation for both customers and wholesalers. Virtual communities will act as agents for their subscribers who will receive adequate, accurate and timely information on products and services; they can purchase at a lower price and with better quality, while this same medium - so supporters claim - meets the social need for communication. The wholesalers will find the virtual community to be a powerful vehicle for expanding their markets, since the very concept is oriented away from brand images.

They will also benefit from the increased propensity of customers to buy, and from reduced marketing costs of customer searching. Wholesalers will also receive a better statistical picture of changing customer tastes and choices and be able to target products to a subset of customers judged more likely to purchase. The virtual community requires a technological strategy based on speed and leverage, with the emphasis on modular technology architecture and a focused information infrastructure. The choice of the network platform is between participation in an online service or the Internet.

The strength of the Internet lies in its enormous diversity of resources assembled in one networking environment, and the TCP/IP and HTML standards offer more opportunity for growth and innovation than proprietary platforms. Widespread developments of new technologies are taking place to make the Internet the best choice for the virtual community.

Thousands of millions of dollars invested in conventional networks, with voice-dominant circuit-switched analog networks, are being threatened by the widespread popularity of the IP-based data networks.

In the local area networks, or LANs, switching technology has resulted in Fast Ethernet in the range of 100 Mb/s and Gigabit Ethernet in the range of 1 Gb/s. Asynchronous Transfer Mode (ATM) has proved useful in full backbone networks as well as in Synchronous Optical Networks (SONETs). According to a worldwide survey conducted by Dell's Oro Group, the market for

ATM switches and concentrators increased by 77% from 1996 to 1997, and 60% from 1997 to 1998.

ATM is also a leader in the MAN/WAN for inter-building and intra-campus connectivity, and is becoming an important infrastructure for public carrier networks. Such ATM networking is bringing significant synergies to the operation of IP networks, allowing for true integration of multiple traffic types on the same network infrastructure. Wireless LANs have strengthened only in areas where optical fibre networks with high bandwidth are either absent or deficient.

Wireless systems have provided good solutions to the last mile problem in MANs. For this, the Multi-channel, Multi-point Distribution System (MDS) in the two GHz band and as the Local Multi-point Distribution System (LMDS) in the high-frequency band between 26 GHz and 30 GHz have found wide acceptance.

With cellular phones, the digitalization process is gaining ground. Trends in Europe are towards the growth of Integrated Services Digital Networks (ISDN), which is not the case in North America. The speed and reliability of ISDN at a typical data transmission rate of 128 Kb/s has made it attractive for homes and small businesses.

Although INMARSAT-A was first launched in 1991 as an alternative to VSATs by offering high transmission speeds from a miniature ground terminal, the latest version called INMARSAT-B Duplex High Speed Data (HSD) service has now become commercially available in all oceanic regions. It supports highspeed file transfer, store and forward video, video conferencing as well as voice, fax and data transmission.

A large number of users including government agencies, international organizations, multinational companies and broadcast service providers have found the services useful. Many of the above-mentioned development, like ATM and SONET, have led to the creation of networked multimedia systems, which offer several advantages for transmitting still and moving images, graphics, texts and sound; a number of content-rich applications are pushing multimedia communications forward.

From the present $9,000 million annual revenue from satellite services, the year 2000 is expected to see nearly $30,000 million. Such Low Earth Orbiting (LEO) Satellite systems (they orbit about 1,000 km above the earth) and Medium Earth Orbit (MEO) satellites will bring about a revolution in global voice, paging and fax systems, as well as usher in the next stage of broad-band multi-satellite systems offering fast Internet and video.

Compared to the $30,000 million invested in the cable television industry over the past two decades, the satellite telecommunications industry has invested more than $20,000 million in the past five years and has lined up $60,000 million for the next five. One of the keys to making satellites pervasive has been the reduction in the cost and size of user terminals by concentrating power more intensely on smaller geographic areas and by reusing precious frequency spectrums many times over.

The growth of the Internet and other distributed networks is making star networks less and less effective. Consequently, in 1997 and 1998, commercial satellites with on-board processing, allowing signals to be switched between spot beams in the satellites, began to appear.

At the beginning of 1997, an estimated 30 million users worldwide used the Web for work, education and recreation at home. With the increase of multimedia applications, Web content is becoming more and more tailored to fast networks.

Web browsers have already become universal Graphical User Interfaces (GUIs) for narrow-band services like e-mail, file transfer, transaction processing, Web surfing, and so on. The technology of the Web browser has been extended to broad-band GUIs.

The strong signalling requirements for networking systems imposed by Web access saw the beginning of a signalling crisis in 1998, because not all network types could comply with the signalling requirements necessary in broad-band systems. One way of solving this problem was to move from pull mode to push mode data. Push mode allows the servers and networks that provide content to make more efficient use of the available bandwidth and processing time.

Voice-over-data and IP Telephoney System

Voice-over-data and IP telephony (VOIP) systems grew exponentially in 1997 and 1998 with a perceptible reduction in telephone tariffs, though at the cost of telephone quality. At present, the IP networks, including the Internet, are not ready for voice-over-data traffic on a very large scale.

While waiting for the advent of broadband Internet-II to offer long term solutions, users will continue to experience the effect of overloading on voice quality. IP telephony includes voice-over LANs, Internet, Intranets and Extranets. Both real-time and store-and-forward fax traffic can also be addressed as can unified messaging over the Web. Personal computers and digital TVs are converging into one integrated product.

Current PCs are constructed with video receiver cards, whereas televisions, with embedded microprocessors required for electronic programme guide (EPG) and digital decoding, have already been built on a pilot scale. Only a small incremental cost is required to add more power and memory to transform a television set into a computer.

Services such as Web TV from Microsoft and Intercast are already narrowing the gap between the Web and television. Efforts are under way to establish a consistent link between the Web television so that broadcasters can create a new form of entertainment.

High Definition TV (HDTV) is a high-quality digital TV development, delivering data services and multiple channels. Super-high definition image system (SHD), with a resolution equal to that of a 35-mm film and data capacity four times that of HDTV, has been introduced to make it possible to read stored newspapers even when they are displayed at actual size. This SHD image system may be combined with a Digital Network Library system to provide versatile applications such as a Digital Museum.

It may be assumed that Web standards will prevail, but adapting Web standards to a purely broadcasting environment is proving difficult. Video on demand (VoD) is an emerging service currently under trial. VoD enables consumers to order films, documentaries and educational broadcast/content over a network. As a pull-mode service, no two subscribers are likely to be watching the same film or using the same VCR control such as 'rewind' and 'fast forward'.

Separate data flows can therefore be established for each viewer using a bandwidth allocated to a single consumer. With digital com-pressionas one of the enabling technologies for VoD with MPEG, a film of television broadcasting quality can be stored in 3 GB of memory and then played out at 3 Mb/s. A variation, called near video on demand (nVoD), is also at the pilot stage. Over the past two years, the set-top-box has gained consumer popularity as a supplement to the televison set.

The set-top-box is used to provide capacity not present in the TV or VCR by including a slot for 'additional functions', along with a tuner appropriate for the transmission medium.

Transmission can be by cable, direct broadcast satellite (DBS), microwave TV, multi-channel, multi-point distribution service (MMDS), cellular TV that uses 28 GHz wireless cable service, or other such devices.

Current services made possible by the set-top-box are navigation and interactive programming systems that use on-screen images and cursor-like devices to allow subscribers to select and interact with other services including home shopping, video on demand, electronic games, educational programmes, electronic publishing and telecommunication services like the Internet. The set-top-box and even television sets have been developed with an embedded network computer (NC).

Whereas networked PCs provide each user with local storage and processing with much of the data located within the mainframe, NC goes a step further by distributing data, programmes and computing power across many nodes on the Internet or Intranets.

Multimedia is situated at the crossroads of a large number and variety of technologies and economic sectors. Furthermore, the industry is developing all the time, and available statistics therefore quickly become unreliable and out of date. This problem is compounded by a lack of coherent definitions, which obscures both factual and conceptual analysis.

In this light, the multimedia revolution is seen to result from the development of the following three types of media:

1) *Computers*: thanks to high-level languages such as Hypertalk, Lingo and Java, multimedia producers no longer need to be computer experts to create documents which combine text, sound and image on a compact disk-read only memory (CD-ROM), CD-Interactive (CD-I), Digital Versatile Disk (DVD) or the Internet.

2) *Digital video*: television is moving towards interactive television (I-TV) and video on demand, offered by cable distribution networks.

3) *Network superhighways* carrying Internet traffic and the information of the future, on which all kinds of interactive services such as electronic mail, voice telephony and videoconferencing, electronic commerce are already flourishing, and soon, perhaps, television on demand.

Hypermedia came into being in the 1980s with the 'Hypertext' of Apple computers, and subsequently spread to all types of data (graphics, fixed images, video sequences, animations, sound) which could be digitized.

But it was the 'hyperdocument', closely identified with a given language and material, which became what we now know as 'multimedia', and applied not only to off-line productions such as CD-ROMs or interactive terminals, but also to applications available on networks and on the Internet in particular.

In multimedia, the computer's main function is no longer calculation, but management, creation and publishing of vast masses of digitized data - both content and services - in text, graphic, audio or audiovisual form. The original media through which these data were transmitted were extremely diverse.

Today, digitized electronic data is the single medium and a computer is the common processing tool. This creates an entirely new environment where the possibilities for creation and use are endless, and probably as yet largely unexplored.

'Multimediation' of data. It may be appropriate here to establish the difference between audiovisual and multimedia material. Audiovisual producers work on documents containing data in several formats, for example image, voice/sound, text and graphics. It is not possible to merge all these data, however, because they are organized differently and use different languages. Producers therefore piece the data together in the form of a 'collage', rather than, accurately speaking, merging them.

Although there is a single basic medium, hypermedia allows a whole range of formats to be used in an integrated manner, from the creation of the product through final use. People who use, consult or work on multimedia products do not do so sequentially, i.e. from start to finish, as when reading a book or watching a film. They move around in this universe of knowledge, guided simply by their intuition, the questions they ask, association of ideas or sensations. They 'navigate' their way around knowledge. The power to navigate in a non-linear fashion, i.e. by association of ideas, within a relational database, is greatly increased by the ability to act at any given moment.

The designers or users of hypermedia products have an ongoing 'dialogue' with the product they are designing/using via their computer. The interactivity of the new systems opens up vast possibilities for human partners who are able to control operations and anticipate results at all times. The provisional definition of multimedia proposed earlier is bound to change rapidly and spread to all media.

The interactive counterparts of the traditional media are flourishing: interactive television, interactive cinema, interactive press, etc. All cultural industries will soon be 'invaded' by multimedia.

Furthermore, everyday the Internet makes further inroads into the areas of commerce, business and industry, resulting in the development of an increasing number of multimedia products such as intranets, extranets, electronic commerce, reference databases, and so on. Multimedia represent one stage in the development of traditional methods for producing, processing, sending and disseminating data.

One of the main characteristics of multimedia is its added value in the case of games, reference works, promotional tools, bank and commercial transactions, training and communication. Multimedia can also be a way of creating innovative concepts. The evolution of supply and demand for these new types of products and services will be closely bound up with technological developments and the adoption of multimedia technologies. All players involved in the multimedia industry are affected by the changes taking place.

There have been a great many acquisitions and mergers; firms have restructured; new players and production companies are springing up all the time; geographical 'areas of excellence' are growing and new products are constantly being developed. The consequences of this constantly-changing market are so great that the usual definitions and data do not adequately reflect the true economics of multimedia.

Instead, they are an illustration of 'imperfect' statistical systems inherited from the past, which have difficulty in keeping up with the changes brought about by the transformation of the media and cultural industries. For this reason, it is important to identify methodological signposts and the market trends. The added value process of today's communications industries is strongly influenced by the impact of multimedia. It may therefore be said to be 'technology-driven'. The market is made up of three main sectors of targeted end-users:

— individuals and consumers,

— companies and economic organizations, and

— institutions.

Multimedia is present in all fields: from the media to the arts, education, consultancy services and museums. However, it is very difficult to pinpoint the extent to which products in these areas can be said to be truly 'multimedia'.

Similarly, it is difficult to estimate the economic weight of multimedia in its various forms. In museums, for example, multimedia may account for only one particular aspect of a specific work or exhibition. The degree of multimedia found in the above-mentioned fields is small but growing, although it is often difficult to determine the percentage of true multimedia activity.

For example, there is multimedia content on the Internet, but the Internet as a whole cannot be said to be multimedia, since at least 80% of its content consists of on-line text, i.e. electronic data in text form. It is very difficult, or even impossible, to determine the exact percentage of true multimedia activity as the concept of interactivity is infinitely elastic, and there is a world of difference between the interactivity of a video recorder and that of a video-game console.

Similarly, although there is much talk now of interactive television, very few households actually possess this technology and, as a result, there are as yet no statistics on the subject.

Multimedia products can be developed on various types of media, such as diskette, CD-ROM, CD-I, DVD-ROM, interactive terminals, and 'closed' or on-line networks. However, they tend to be grouped into two broader categories: on-line media and off-line applications.

On-line products can be consulted via telephone networks, cable or broadband networks known as 'information superhighways' such as the Internet. Different sources of information on sales of multimedia products and services all show a marked increase in the income generated by this sector since the beginning of the 1990s, and this increase is set to continue over the next ten years.

The international study by Frost and Sullivan—World Multimedia Application Market—points to a significant increase in this sector. The overall growth in the market is reflected both in the demand for products on optical media and in the use of on-line services. The demand for multimedia products is mainly concentrated in North America, where in 1994 sales of applications totalled approximately $4,000 million—nearly 50% of world sales.

However, the share of international revenue generated by the American market will decrease over time to the advantage of other geographical regions, in particular the Pacific. Demand for multimedia products and services is currently measured in terms of the use of optical discs, since this is the most common support medium used for multimedia products and services. Worldwide sales of CD-ROMs (databases, images, sound and multimedia) totalled 8 million units in 1993, 16.5 million in 1994 and 53.9 million in 1995.

The number of CD-ROMs available on the market also showed a staggering increase of 800% between 1990 and 1995, yielding an average annual growth rate of 51%. It should be said that multimedia productions in 1995 accounted for only 25% of the total number of CD-ROMs in circulation (75% of all CD-ROMs presumably contained other data).

The United States is the main geographical market for multimedia applications. In 1994, 55% of all optical disk drives were used in the United States, compared to 19% in Japan, 14% in Europe and 12% in the rest of the world. The enthusiasm for multimedia applications has also led to a significant rise in demand for on-line services, especially for data communications networks and direct-access databases.

The Internet is the main data communications network on a world scale, and links some 100,000 networks in more than two hundred countries. The explosion of this network has created a huge market of users of multimedia products. Unfortunately there are no reliable data on the subject. It is very difficult to compare differences and similarities between different countries regarding the use of multimedia products with any accuracy owing to the lack of reliable data and clear definitions at present.

Role of the Internet

In the world, most people who encounter the Internet consider it to be a vibrant medium of exchange that supports a wide variety of uses, most of them commercial.

Many also know that, having been created with support from the United States Government, Defence Advanced Research Project Agency (DARPA) initially, and later the National Science Foundation (NSF), the Department of Education (DOE) and other agencies and departments, the Internet has its roots in the research and development community. In recent years, the private sector has made extensive investments in building Internet capabilities, and its recent growth has been almost entirely fuelled by such private sector initiatives. However, as recently as a decade ago, the Internet was still the private enclave of the research and education community.

At that time, few in the telecommunications business believed that the private sector would come to play such a critical role in leading its continued development and that the Internet would come to play such a central role in the United States (and indeed the world's) economy in the short span of ten years. The Internet is a collection of networks around the world that inter-operate seamlessly via an open architecture and its associated protocols.

The first three networks in the Internet were the Advanced Research Project Agency Network (ARPANET), packet radio network, and packet satellite network, all sponsored by DARPA several decades ago. Each of these three networks was individually designed and implemented, but most importantly, the Internet architecture was created to be independent of the detailed design or implementation of any of its constituent networks. As a result, the technology for networking could evolve and change, and the latest technology could be integrated with the prior technology simply by adding new networks.

The success of the Internet was therefore heavily dependent on the underlying computer communications technology that had been pioneered in the ARPANET. The basic notions of packet switching were already well known by the late 1960s and had been successfully demonstrated in the ARPANET project by the early 1970s. To get to the Internet architecture was not a completely straightforward path, however, from the early network developments.

In fact, the original implementation of the packet satellite network equipment assumed it would be integrated into upper memory of an ARPANET IMP (Interface Message Processors), and not be a separate, externally accessible network. This was perhaps the first of many cases where the network management required close co-ordination with network architecture and raised the basic issue of overall governance of the 'network of networks'.

Although the Internet was growing at 100% per year prior to 1993, the introduction of the Mosaic browser for the World Wide Web caused usage of the Internet to accelerate dramatically. It is now widely assumed that, by the end of this decade, approximately 100 million users will have access to the Internet. While the decision by the United States Government to privatize key parts of the Internet, such as the Domain Name System (DNS), became embroiled in debate across many continents, this is not a new phenomenon.

In working with the Internet Society and various diverse groups from many quarters, it recognized the role that private-sector bodies had to play in the overall organization and governance of the Internet. The notion of fairness is likely to be elusive among competing parties, and, left to their own devices, private sector organizations will be more inclined to tilt the process in their own favour whenever possible.

For businesses, where the investments can be shared among many users and considered as a business expense, the situation is more manageable, but there is little incentive to make these investments unless the traffic or the applications demand it. If inexpensive local access with consumption-based pricing of long-haul services can be provided, then high-speed capabilities may become affordable for businesses. Computer and software companies will then have an incentive to produce the needed hardware and software for gigabit applications.

The rapid growth of paging, cellular telephony and other wireless applications (including wireless Local Area Networks, or LANs, and Internet access) have caused the prices for wireless devices to drop almost to the level of commodities. Palm-sized devices with computing capabilities approaching those of full desktop PCs (but with limited display, storage and battery life) have recently emerged and will eventually dominate the market.

E-mail

E-mail has been a fixture on the network since the earliest days of the ARPAN ET, as have computer files and the ability to move them between machines on the network. The World Wide Web has greatly simplified the mechanics of specifying files as a single string (known as a Uniform Resource Locator, or URL) consisting of the machine name followed by the file name.

Furthermore, the Web design took some of the best features of Standard General Markup Language (SGML), a graphics markup language pioneered by the publishing community, and produced a simplified version called HTML that was easier to learn.

Files written in HTML could be more easily manipulated by computer for presentation on many screens than could files formatted in many different, perhaps even arbitrary ways. Many users connect to the Internet simply to send and receive e-mail and to access the Web. These two functions are a first important step in making digital information available on the Internet.

Recent efforts to create repositories of digital objects that can persist over long periods of time and that can be accessed with precision through sophisticated search mechanisms are almost within reach. These systems, part of an open-architecture approach known generally as 'digital object infrastructure', have the ability to encompass the Web as well as most other information systems. The future rarely plays out the way we imagine it will, and in the full knowledge that any such predictions are likely to be disproved by practice, the following possibilities may nonetheless be proposed.

E-commerce will continue to flourish, with a move away from prepackaged buying options prepared by sellers, to more opportunities for customization and other user-defined products and services.

Intermediate organizations on the Internet will find better ways to match the needs of potential customers and suppliers of goods and services. Better means for locating all kinds of items will be developed, including the ability to locate individuals (primarily those who wish to be found, but possibly some who do not), to locate sources of goods of all kinds including new and used components, and even to trace the history and performance of selected goods and services.

Building worldwide markets is largely a nontechnical problem, but technology can greatly assist in this domain. The organization of marketing forces on the Internet is still in its infancy and will probably only increase in sophistication over time.

Virtually all school and district level decision-makers now have access to electronic information. Over 95% of schools have computers connected to the Internet and local area networks. The infrastructure is in place, then, to profoundly improve access to decision-support information about educational goals, standards, and performance.

Throughout the nation, states and districts are using this IT infrastructure to do just that. The typical web-based EDI concerning educational standards and school performance. The information moves electronically instead of in cartons in trucks, and can be revised without incurring large re-distribution costs. The web-based information is intended for anyone with an interest in the performance of schools in a given locale or in the performance of a particular school.

Teachers, principals, and parents can evaluate the performance of their school in relation to standards and in relation to the performance of other schools; school board members, civic leaders, and policymakers can evaluate the performance of groups of schools in which they have an interest.

The information reveals how well students are achieving in schools, identifies needs for improvement, and depending upon the quality of the measurements, which schools are performing adequately and which schools are not. This creates a more efficient and rational basis for instructional management decision-making, and for allocating rewards, sanctions, and resources aimed at school improvement. Before computer networking and electronic information exchange, performance data on schools was locked exclusively into paper reports that moved slowly through the organization, typically down the organizational hierarchy, from one office to the next. At the school level, administrators would typically have responsibility for disseminating test results among school faculty–a process carried out in a wide variety of ways, with widely varying efficiency, and often involving a lot of photo-copying.

And the revolution in information technology brought to schools networked information systems that have given teachers and administrators much improved access to information on curriculum standards, school performance reports, and student and school profile characteristics.

3

Educational Development Worldwide

During the year 1999, the availability of technology in the classroom was related to teachers' use of that technology. Additionally, teachers who had more computers available in the classroom were generally more likely to report assigning students to use computers or the Internet to a large extent to conduct various tasks. In US, National Assessment of Educational Progress (NAEP) teacher survey, and the Current Population Survey (CPS) from 1994 to 1998. Data are also provided from the 1994 to 1999 FRSS school surveys on the percent of schools and instructional rooms with Internet connections.

Measures of computer availability come in a variety of forms, including the percent of students who have varying numbers of computers available to them in their schools (NAEP), student-to-computer ratios in schools (FRSS), the percent of students who have computer labs and portable computers available to them (NAEP), the percent of students who have computers permanently available in the classroom (NAEP), and the percent of students for whom computers are best described as available in computer labs or available in the classroom (NAEP). Measures of Internet availability in public schools are similar, but typically focus on the percent of schools connected to the Internet rather than on the percent of students with the Internet available to them.

These measures include the percent of schools connected to the Internet Availability of Technology for Instructional Purposes. Number of computers available to students and student-to-computer ratios. Beginning in 1990, NAEP began collecting data from school administrators on the number of computers available to students in the school.

Results from these surveys demonstrate a substantial increase in the number of computers available to public school students in their schools between 1990 and 1999. For example, the percent of fourth-grade students who had more than 76 computers available in their schools rose from 1 percent in 1990 to 33 percent in 1998. Similarly, there was an increase from 8 percent to 51 percent of eighth-grade students and from 42 percent to 73 percent of twelfth-grade students during those years.

According to recent FRSS data, approximately one computer was available for every six students in 1999. Computer availability in labs and classrooms. Data are also available from the NAEP 1998 school survey on the location of computers in the school. For example, administrators indicated if the school had computer labs and whether computers were always available in classrooms.

Additionally, administrators were asked if computers were available to be brought to classrooms for student use as a measure of portable computer availability. The different types of computer availability (e.g., labs, available to be brought to class, classrooms) varied by grade-level in 1998.

For example, among public school students, eighth and twelfth-grade students were more likely than fourth-grade students to have computer labs available. Conversely, fourth-grade students were more likely to have computers always available in the classroom than eighth and twelfth-grade students. Teachers' reports of computer availability to students.

In 1998, public school teachers of fourth-and eighth-grade students were asked to best describe the availability of computers for use by their students. Teachers reported whether: computers were "not available to students anywhere," computers for student use were "available in a lab," or varying numbers of computers for student use were "available in class." According to their teachers, the majority of both fourth-grade and eighth-grade students had computers available to them somewhere in their school in 1998, either in the classroom or elsewhere in the school. Specifically, percent of fourth-grade students and 49 percent of eighth-grade students had at least one computer in their classrooms, and 23 percent of fourth-grade students and 42 percent of eighth-grade students had at least one computer available in lab.

Thus, 5 percent of fourth-graders and 9 percent of eighth-graders did not have computers available in their schools. The FRSS also collected data on the percent of public schools and instructional rooms that were connected to the Internet as part of its school surveys between 1994 and 1999. In 1994, a little over a third of all public schools were connected to the Internet. By 1999, availability had grown to 95 percent, with one computer connected to the Internet for every 9 students.

The percent of instructional rooms connected to the Internet grew even more sharply during that time—whereas 3 percent of instructional rooms were connected to the Internet in 1994, 63 percent were connected by 1999. The 1999 FRSS data indicate differences in student-to-instructional-computer ratios by such school characteristics as enrolment size, location, poverty concentration, and minority enrollments.

For example, the smallest schools had a lower student-to-instructional-computer ratio than medium and large schools (4 compared with 6 each), as well as a lower student-to-instructional-computer-with- Internet ratio. Rural schools had a lower student-to-instructional-computer ratio than schools in other locations. Furthermore, rural schools had lower student-to-instructional-computer-with-Internet ratios than urban fringe and city schools. Additionally, there were differences in student-to-instructional-computer ratios by poverty concentration and minority enrollments in 1999. Similarly, schools with the highest minority enrollments had a higher student-to-instructional-computer ratio than schools with lower minority enrollments.

Differences by poverty concentration and minority enrollments were also present in student-to-instructional-computer-with-Internet ratios. Schools with more than 70 percent of students eligible for free or reduced-price lunch had more students per instructional computer with Internet than schools with lower poverty concentrations.

Similarly, schools with the highest minority enrollments had a higher student-to-instructional-computer-with- Internet ratio than schools with lower minority enrollments. The highest poverty schools were also less likely to report having instructional rooms connected to the Internet than several other groups in 1997 and 1998. Between 1998 and 1999, all schools except those with the highest poverty concentrations reported an increase in the percentage of instructional rooms connected to the Internet.

In 1999, 39 percent of instructional rooms at schools with more than 70 percent of students eligible for free or reduced-price lunch were connected to the Internet, compared with 62 to 74 percent of schools with lower concentrations of poverty. The availability of computers in teachers' homes is compared with that of adults in other occupations, and the number and ages of computers in the home are also given for the most recent year. Results from the 1994 to 1998 CPS indicate that the availability of computers in public and private school teachers' homes increased significantly between 1994 and 1998.

Furthermore, elementary and secondary teachers were more likely to have a computer at home than adults in all other occupations in 1994 through 1998. Additionally, in 1998, most teachers and adults in other occupations reported having computers that were three years old or newer. The CPS also collected data on public and private school students' computer availability at home in 1994 to 1998.

According to these data, the percent of students who had at least one computer in the home increased from 36 percent in 1994 to 56 percent in 1998. Finally, the relationship between computer availability in the classroom and teachers' computer-related activities is explored. Nearly all public school teachers reported having computers available somewhere in their schools in 1999.

Eighty-four percent of public school teachers had computers available in their classrooms, and 95 percent of teachers had computers available elsewhere in the school. Number of computers in the classroom. In addition to asking teachers if they had computers available in the classrooms, the 1999 FRSS survey also asked for the number of computers available in the classroom.

Thirty-six percent had one computer in their classrooms, 38 percent reported having two to five computers in their classrooms, and 10 percent reported having more than five computers in their classrooms. Differences in school and classroom computer availability by school characteristics. Teachers' computer availability in 1999 varied by several school characteristics, including instructional level, enrolment size, location, minority enrollments, and poverty concentration.

Elementary teachers were more likely to have computers in their classrooms than secondary teachers. Teachers in schools enrolling less than 300 and 300 to 999 students were more likely to have computers in their classrooms than teachers in schools with the largest enrollments. Last, teachers in schools with 21 to 49 percent minority enrollments were more likely to have computers in the classroom than teachers in schools with 50 percent or more minority enrollments.

There were also differences among teachers who had varying numbers of computers in the classroom. Not only were some groups of teachers less likely to have computers in their classrooms, but they were also more likely than other teachers to have only one computer in their classrooms. Teachers in secondary schools were more likely to have one computer than elementary teachers, and less likely to have two to five computers than elementary teachers. Computer availability also varied by school size.

For example, teachers in schools enrolling 1,000 or more students were more likely to report having one computer in their classrooms than teachers in schools with less than 300 students. Teachers in schools enrolling 1,000 or more students were less likely, however, to report having two to five computers than either schools enrolling 300 to 999 students or schools enrolling less than 300 students. Sixty-four percent of public school teachers who reported having computers in their classrooms also reported having Internet availability in their classrooms in 1999.

Ninety percent of teachers who reported having computers available elsewhere in their schools also reported that the Internet was available elsewhere in the school. Number of classroom computers connected to the Internet. Among the teachers who reported having computers available in their classrooms, approximately one-third had no computers connected to the Internet and about half had one computer connected to the Internet.

It was less commonly reported that teachers had two to five computers connected or more than five computers connected to the Internet. Differences in school and classroom Internet availability by school characteristics. There were differences in overall Internet availability (in class or elsewhere in the school) and in the number of classroom computers connected to the Internet by several school characteristics.

For example, secondary teachers with computers in their classrooms were more likely to have Internet availability in their classrooms than elementary teachers. Internet available on the computers that they did have in their classrooms.

Furthermore, among teachers who reported having computers available elsewhere in the school, secondary teachers were also more likely to have Internet availability elsewhere in the school than were elementary teachers. Additionally, teachers in schools located in towns were more likely to have Internet availability elsewhere in the school than teachers in urban fringe schools or city schools. Similarly, teachers in schools with lower minority enrollments were generally more likely to report this availability elsewhere in the school than teachers in schools with the highest minority enrollments. Internet availability also varied by poverty concentration.

For example, public school teachers in schools where 11 to 30 percent and 31 to 49 percent of the students qualify for free or reduced-price lunch were more likely to have the Internet available in the classroom than teachers in schools with 71 percent or more students eligible. Teachers in lower poverty schools were also generally more likely than teachers in the highest poverty schools to have Internet available elsewhere in the school.

Specifically, teachers in schools with less than 11 percent, 11 to 30 percent, and 31 to 49 percent students eligible for free or reduced-price lunch were more likely to have this availability than teachers in schools with 71 percent or more students eligible. As with overall

Internet availability in the classroom, the number of classroom computers that public school teachers reported as having Internet connections varied by instructional level and minority enrollments, but not percent of students eligible for free or reduced-price lunch.

For example, secondary teachers were more likely than elementary teachers to have either one computer connected to the Internet or more than five computers connected. In addition, teachers in schools with 6 to 20 percent minority enrollments were more likely than teachers in schools with 50 percent or more minority enrollments to have one computer connected to the Internet. Moreover, teachers in schools with less than 6 percent minority enrollments were more likely to report having two to five computers connected than teachers in schools with 50 percent or more minority enrollments.

Rural teachers were more likely to report e-mail availability than city teachers. Moreover, teachers in schools with lower minority enrollments were more likely to report that e-mail was available than teachers in schools with the highest minority enrollments. Furthermore, teachers in schools with less than 11 percent, 11 to 30 percent, and 31 to 49 percent students eligible for free or reduced-price lunch were more likely to have e-mail available than teachers in schools with more than 70 percent eligible students. Teachers in urban fringe schools and schools located in towns were more likely to have the Internet available at home. Teachers in schools with the highest minority enrollments were less likely to report that the majority of their students had computers at home than teachers in any other schools.

In addition, teachers in the lower poverty schools were more likely to report that their students had computers at home than teachers in the highest poverty schools. Teachers' reports of assigning students to use computers or the Internet for various instructional purposes differed by the number of computers in their classrooms. For example, 59 percent of teachers with one computer in the classroom reported not assigning students to use computers or the Internet to solve problems or analyze data, compared with 40 percent of teachers with two to five computers and 23 percent of teachers with more than five computers.

Use of Technology in Schools

In the 1999 FRSS teacher survey, public school teachers were asked if computers, the Internet, and e-mail were available to them in various locations, and if available, the extent to which they used them. Among teachers who reported that computers were available in their schools, 99 percent indicated that they used computers either in their classrooms or elsewhere in the school. Additionally, among teachers who indicated that computers with Internet connections were available in their schools, 96 percent used the Internet from their classrooms or elsewhere in their schools. Furthermore, at least three-fourths of teachers with e-mail availability used it at school. Frequency of use by location of technology.

The 1999 FRSS teacher survey asked teachers how frequently they used computers and the Internet in two locations: the classroom and elsewhere in the school. Of the teachers who reported having computer availability in their classrooms, nearly all of them.

In addition, among teachers with Internet availability in their classrooms, 88 percent reported using this technology. Of those teachers who reported Internet availability elsewhere in the school, 70 percent indicated using it. Teachers were more likely to use the Internet in the classroom than elsewhere in the school, and they were also more likely to use it to a large extent in their classrooms than elsewhere in the school. Furthermore, of the 74 percent of teachers reporting e-mail availability in the school, 77 percent used it at least to some extent. Teachers were significantly more likely to use computers in the classroom than elsewhere in the school, and they were also more likely to use them to a large extent in the classroom than elsewhere in the school.

Frequency of use by number of computers available. The 1999 FRSS teacher survey also asked teachers the number of computers and computers with Internet connections that were located in their classrooms. Overall, teachers with more computers in their classrooms used them more frequently than teachers with fewer computers in their classrooms.

For example, 62 percent of public school teachers with more than five computers in their classrooms used them to a large extent compared with 43 percent of teachers with two to five computers and 28 percent of teachers with one computer in their classrooms.

Similarly, teachers with more than five computers with Internet access in their classrooms used the Internet from the classroom more frequently than teachers with fewer computers with Internet access in their

Furthermore, teachers with computers in their classrooms used computers elsewhere in the school more often than teachers with no classroom computers. At least one-fifth of teachers with computers in their classrooms used computers elsewhere in the school to a large extent compared with 10 percent of teachers with no computers in their classrooms. Similarly, teachers with one or more than five computers connected to the Internet in their classrooms used the Internet elsewhere in the school more often than teachers without classroom computers with Internet connections.

Twenty-four percent of teachers with more than five classroom computers connected to the Internet and 12 percent of teachers with one classroom computer connected to the Internet used the Internet elsewhere in the school to a large extent, compared with 7 percent of teachers with no classroom computers connected to the Internet.

Frequency of use by teacher and school characteristics. Differences were found in the frequency of teachers' use of computers, the Internet, and e-mail by school and teacher characteristics. Teachers with fewer years of teaching experience were more likely to use computers, the Internet, and e-mail to a large extent at school than their more experienced colleagues.

For example, 48 percent of teachers with 3 or fewer years of teaching experience and 45 percent of teachers with 4 to 9 years of experience used computers at school to a large extent, compared with 33 percent of teachers with 20 or more years experience. The pattern is similar for Internet and e-mail use. Furthermore, teachers in schools with minority enrolments of 6 to 20 percent were more likely to use e-mail to a large extent than teachers in schools with the highest minority enrolments.

According to the 1997 CPS, 69 percent of adults employed as secondary teachers (either in public or private schools) and 67 percent employed as elementary teachers (either in public or private schools) reported using computers at work. Both arc significantly lower than such occupations as librarians, editors and reporters, and college faculty, and the percentage of elementary school teachers who reported using computers at work was lower than that of those employed as lawyers and judges and real estate and available in the classroom" analyses.

Teachers who reported that computers with Internet connections were not available to them in the classroom were excluded from the "Number of computers with Internet connections available in the classroom" analyses. In the 1999 FRSS teacher survey, public school teachers were asked how often students in one of their typical classes used computers and the Internet—"not at all," "rarely," "sometimes," or "often"—in various locations (i.e., in classrooms and elsewhere in the school).

— *Overall technology use*: Eighty-eight percent of teachers with computers available in their schools reported that their students used computers either in the classroom or in computer labs, libraries, and media centres in 1999.

— *Frequency of use by location of technology*: Approximately seven out of ten teachers reported that students used classroom computers; however, a higher percentage of teachers reported that students used them elsewhere in the school. Thirty-four percent of teachers reported that students used the Internet in the classroom; however, a higher percentage of teachers reported that students used the Internet elsewhere in the school. Twenty-six percent of teachers reported that students used classroom computers often, and 28 percent of teachers reported that students used computers elsewhere often. Six percent of teachers indicated that students used classroom computers with Internet access often, and percent of teachers indicated that students used computers with Internet access elsewhere in the school often.

Sixteen percent of teachers reported that students used other technologies, such as distance learning 3 through the Internet and other interactive media. Frequency of use by number of computers available. Overall, teachers with more computers or Internet availability in their classrooms reported that they and their students used these technologies more frequently than teachers with fewer computers in their classrooms. Similarly, 33 percent of teachers with more than five classroom computers connected to the Internet reported that students used them often compared with 6 percent of teachers with one classroom computer connected to the Internet.

Additionally, teachers with two to five classroom computers connected to the Internet were more likely than teachers with one such computer to report that students used the Internet often. Furthermore, teachers with computers in their classrooms reported that students used computers elsewhere in the school more often than teachers with no classroom computers. At least one out of three teachers with computers in their classrooms reported that students used computers elsewhere in the school, compared with one out of six teachers without a classroom computer.

Teachers with more than five computers connected to the Internet in their classrooms were two to five times as likely as teachers with one or no computers with Internet connections to report that students used the

Internet elsewhere in the school. Additionally, teachers with one, two to five, and more than five computers with Internet access in the classroom were more likely than teachers with no computers with Internet access in the classroom to report that their students used the Internet elsewhere in the school. Frequency of use by teacher and school characteristics.

Students' use of technology, as reported by their teachers, varied by teacher and school characteristics. For example, elementary teachers were more likely than secondary teachers to report that their students used computers at school to any extent. However, secondary teachers were more likely than elementary teachers to report that their students used the Internet at school to any extent. Furthermore, teachers in schools with lower minority enrolments were generally more likely than teachers in schools with the highest minority enrolments to report that students used the Internet at school.

Sixty-four percent of teachers in schools with less than 6 percent minority enrolments and 65 percent of teachers in schools with 6 to 20 percent minority enrolments reported that students used the Internet in school compared with 53 percent of teachers in schools with more than 50 percent minority enrolments.

Similarly, teachers in schools with lower poverty concentrations were generally more likely to report that students used the Internet at school than teachers in the highest poverty schools. In the 1999 FRSS teacher survey of technology use, teachers were asked if a computer, the Internet, or a school network through which they could access the Internet were available to them at home. If they were available, teachers were then asked about the extent to which they used them.

Because the FRSS did not ask similar information about students, data from NAEP and CPS are used to describe students' technology use at home. The 1997 CPS indicates that for public and private school teachers, 83 percent of elementary teachers and 89 percent of secondary teachers used home computers to any extent when they were available. This compares with 74 percent of adults in other occupations with computers at home who used them to any extent.

Two years later, the 1999 FRSS teacher survey indicates that 98 percent of public school teachers with computers at home used them, and about half of the teachers used them to a large extent. Teachers' Internet use at home significantly increased between 1997 and 1998 for both elementary and secondary teachers. According to the 1997 CPS, 35 percent of all elementary teachers with computers in their households and 44 percent of all secondary teachers with computers in their households reported using the Internet at home. Home Internet use also increased between 1997 and 1998 for adults in other occupations with computers in their households, from 37 to 51 percent.

The 1999 FRSS teacher survey indicates that nearly all public school teachers with the Internet available at home used it, and about two-fifths of teachers with home Internet access reported using it to a large extent. The 1999 FRSS teacher survey also inquired about school networks that teachers can access at home. Fifty-six percent of teachers used this technology when it was available. Home use by teacher and school characteristics.

Public school teachers' use of computers and the Internet at home varied by their years of teaching experience. For example, teachers with 3 or fewer years and those with 4 to 9 years of teaching experience were more likely to use their home computers to a large extent than teachers with 20 or more years of teaching experience.

Similarly, teachers with 3 or fewer years and those with 4 to 9 years of teaching experience were more likely to use the Internet at home to a large extent than teachers with 10 to 19 years and those with 20 or more years of teaching experience. Public school teachers who used computers for instruction during class and teachers who assigned projects that required their students to use a computer were more likely to use computers and the Internet at home to a large extent than teachers who did not use these technologies for such purposes.

For example, 54 percent of teachers who used computers for instruction also used home computers to a large extent, compared with 43 percent of teachers who did not use computers for instruction. Likewise, 52 percent of teachers who assigned projects requiring students to use computers also used home computers to a large extent, compared with 37 percent of teachers who did not assign such projects. Every revolutionary technology starts with a whimper. Its full revolutionary bang is realized only later after fundamental structural changes are made to accommodate the new technology. Steam engines were first put on sailboats to solve a persistent problem: time wasted in the doldrums.

When there was no wind, the steam engine was fired up and used only until there was enough wind for sailing. Steam was initially viewed as a solution to a problem for sailboats, not as a replacement for them. But, of course, in the end sail power vanished and steam permitted faster, larger, safer, all-metal ships that could move goods faster and much more economically. There are countless examples like these in the history of technology, where a new technology is first used to address a narrow problem within the existing order and only later overthrew the old order.

The delay is inevitable because structural changes are needed for the new technology. In the case of ice machines, universal access to electricity and lower costs through mass production were needed before everyone could buy a refrigerator. In the case of steamboats, deeper harbors, new construction techniques, and railroads to supply coal and remove cargoes were needed before large, steel steamers made sense.

There is dawning realization that the current economic boom has technology to thank because of the structural changes it has caused in business. Productivity is up because technology means that fewer managers are needed, businesses are far less hierarchical, and financial markets have been democratized. In spite of the decades that computers have been around and their current high use in schools, we have yet to see the revolution they could cause in learning.

Educators are still delivering block ice made by ice machines, still using steam only in the doldrums. This is because business competition rewards improvements while education is organized to conserve and pass on the best of the old. In addition, education is highly labor-intensive, and the cost of labor has been bid up by the buoyant economy. Before jumping into the specifics of the educational change that technology will cause, it is important to understand where we are in the information revolution and where it is going.

The Law of Moore's

"Moore's Law", an observation made by Gordon Moore in 1965, several years before helping start Intel. Moore observed then that the number of transistors on a microchip was doubling every 18 months. This kind of exponential change applies to the entire information industry, not just computer chips. Similar exponential increases in performance will be seen in all components: displays, keyboards, and media. Experts expect these changes to continue 10-20 more years, but no one really knows.

The result might be a trillion-fold increase in performance since 1965 and a million-fold increase from today. It is impossible to predict what new applications that these improvements in the underlying technology will enable, but it is certain that the structural changes necessary to exploit them fully in education will take additional decades. A direct consequence of the ongoing revolution described above, in only a few years computers will be very inexpensive and ubiquitous. Each person will own several and have easy access to more—all able to communicate over the Internet.

Toys, TVs, phones, pagers, handhelds, and general-purpose computers will have access to the net. Wireless access will become common and switching between wired and wireless connections will be effortless. Any indicator of technology access in the U.S. will show a similar behavior over the next decade, showing a gap that dwindles into insignificance as prices drop.

This is because information technologies are relatively low-cost and dropping. Unlike jets, reactors, and rockets, computer and network technologies are "democratic technologies." Like TVs, VCRs, calculators, and radios, information technologies are soon to be ubiquitous. The vanishing of the digital divide defined as access to technology in the U.S. will not, of course, rectify the deplorable inequities in U.S. schools.

Because of inadequate funding and more difficult working conditions, too many poor schools will not use the technology well, will be unable to maintain it, and will provide fewer opportunities for their teachers to exploit it. The result will be continued poorer education in many poorer schools. The cost of access to technology will not contribute significantly to this persistent, essentially political, problem. If anything, the technology, by providing free access to increasingly valuable resources, will have a leveling effect that will tend to reduce the gap. The situation throughout the world will be essentially similar, with the exception of much of central Africa.

In most parts of the world, the huge digital divides that exist today will close as access becomes ubiquitous. Many countries already exceed the U.S. access to technology and even developing countries see the importance of computer and networking technologies. Ubiquity will be accompanied by increasing reliance on the network to synchronize data. You want your personal mailing list to be on your cell phone and TV computer. If your student masters multi-digit subtraction in school, her educational games at home should take advantage of this and her parents should be informed.

Data collected on a colleague's handheld computer should be available on your portable. All these feats of synchronization will happen automatically and effortlessly through the network. The location of the data will not matter; you may choose to store your data on your main computer's hard drive, a server in Budapest, or for security, your personal smart card. It is quite likely that each learner will have a net-based educational profile that can change as the individual learns.

This is how a student's progress can be monitored, shared among different computers she uses, and reported, as appropriate, to parents and others responsible for her education. Leapfrog, a maker of educational toys, is already planning a line of mass-produced products based on this principle. An online educational profile is a potential privacy bombshell.

Everyone will want tight and secure control over who looks at grades, test scores, progress, weaknesses, essays, and preferences. Technology can solve this, though, through some combination of encryption, a smart card that physically controls the data, and related software.

These characteristics have led to the Internet's impact on commerce and have dictated the structural changes needed to exploit fully the technology in business. We can look at these for hints about the similar structural changes needed in education. The power of the Internet is that almost anyone can contribute to it and there are ways to find anyone's contribution. This could lead to the junk and misinformation drowning the relatively rare pearls.

This is unlikely, however, because the decentralization also supports self-appointed annotators and collectors of links that provide vetting and review functions. In fact, this self-publishing feature has unleashed tremendous human creativity. Every corporation, government agency, school, town, association, group, museum, and individual wants to put their best on the net. One of the most dramatic manifestations of the ethic of sharing that the Internet has spawned "open source".

The open source movement is highly decentralized, but rallies around the idea of the GNU Public License (GPL) as an alternative to conventional copyright protection. The GPL states that anyone can use the source code without charge providing the user protect any improvements with the GPL license. Companies can sell the software, providing that they continue to make the source freely available. The result is that the source code stays public and keeps getting refined.

GPL software can be better than software simply placed in the public domain, because the terms of the GNU license stop anyone from grabbing the public code and making it proprietary. The result is code that everyone is motivated to review and improve the code. Code that survives tends to be lean, elegant, stable, and free. Initially, open source software focused on the Linux operating system software, but this is changing rapidly.

The people shaping the effort insist that system software is only the beginning. Because open source development is the best way to create reliable and elegant software, they are certain that most software will eventually be distributed under the GPL. The open source motto is "Software is meant to be free." They may be right. Already the open source idea has reached far beyond Linux.

In addition to the Netscape browser, there are now open source spreadsheets, word processors, a presentation package (like PowerPoint), and gimp, an image manipulation program that is better than PhotoShop. The open source software idea is beginning to appeal to corporations, because it offers an inexpensive way to incorporate free software into their product and get better product support than they can afford to hire.

All Netscape's code is open source, as is much of the next generation Macintosh operating system. IBM is installing GNU/Linux into some computers. The U.S. has led the world in Internet use and implementation, but the rest of the world will overtake. The largest growth in Internet use over the next few years is expected in Latin America and Asia. According to Global Reach, currently, 49% of the 335 million Internet users worldwide are non-English speaking. In 2003, the 670 million non-English users will be more than double the number of English-speaking users.

There are already 18 million Chinese users and there might be 125 million in 2003. While these projections are open to question, the general trend is not. The majority of the educated population of the world along with most of its institutions will be strutting their stuff online in a few years. These new users will bring a rich collection of new resources and interests to everyone. The world's books, art, data, pictures, animations, music, simulations, poems, and much more will be available.

Collaborators, collectors, mentors, advisors, and consultants for every imaginable topic will be a few clicks away. Unfortunately, all kinds of undesirable resources will also be increasingly available. There will be the entire world's junk, smut, hatred, violence, stupidity, superstition, and insanity. Every form of vice and bad habit will be represented, too.

Even more viruses will be circulated and more attacks on computer systems mounted. In addition, the Internet is rapidly becoming commercialized. Some of the most amazing services are available free, subsidized by advertisers. Computers, email, storage, faxing, news, music, search engines, financial data, and much more are available free because they are paid for by advertisers.

There is no point in avoiding the Internet because of these undesirable aspects. We have to face the problems and learn to minimize them. One of the skills we will need to learn is how to find the good, reliable stuff for ourselves and youngsters in our charge while avoiding the bad. Software tools have revolutionized business and hold the key to breakthroughs in education as well.

Software tools are general-purpose, flexible applications that you can apply to your specific needs. In business, spreadsheets, presentation software, and communication tools have empowered workers to make decisions and marshal resources without the need of levels of hierarchy. Design tools have sped the development of new devices and software, increasing productivity. In education, tool applications will also lead increases in learning and productivity in all disciplines.

Literacy tools are revolutionizing the language arts, design tools have broad application across the arts and engineering, and conceptual tools will completely change all technical and social science learning.

For a tool to be educational, it needs to be part of an instructional design. Software can help there, too, especially if the tool and pedagogy are separated. All these new tools will be too expensive to develop from grants and corporate investments but open source can solve this problem. Technological tools will become increasingly important in teaching literacy and second languages to children, adults, and special students.

Over the next few years, there could be important breakthroughs in technology-enhanced literacy learning, because there is a convergence of developments: Voice recognition. Research is underway on computer recognition of children's voices and speakers with accents. This ability can be used to recognize reading, judge accuracy, and shape pronunciation. The coming inexpensive ubiquitous computers will give all learners could access to inexpensive literacy tools.

Students can use networks to find an audience for their work, a community of interest and collaborators for their investigations. Game machine quality simulations. The incredible graphics capacity of new 128-bit game computers may create the emotional impact that can capture any learner's imagination. Computer generated material can continuously evaluate student reading and writing, reducing wasted testing time. Inexpensive handhelds will soon be able to exploit these developments to provide interactive voice generation and recognition.

With embedded assessment, the material can advance as fast or slowly as the learner needs. Playful content will be available for young readers while vocationally-relevant material will better suit adults. While human intervention, motivation, and supervision will be necessary, the ubiquitous technology and software tools will greatly reduce the amount of teacher time required for literacy instruction. The bulk of the reading, listening, and correcting can be shifted to the computer, resulting in huge productivity breakthroughs.

This could result in literacy gains worldwide, while decreasing the advantage families have that can find the time to read to their children extensively. Software tools that support creativity are one of the great gifts of computers.

Design tools for Web development, robot programming, and music composition are available and increasingly used in education. Design as a subject is under-represented in schools today. Design is at the core of engineering, architecture, many technologies, and art. The success of many businesses depends on their technical and artistic designs. Successful designs depend on planning, testing, knowledge, and artistic sensibilities.

A central goal of education should be to foster these skills. Perhaps the root of the lack of emphasis on design education has been a perception that design consists of two parts that each seem to be problematic. Its creative side has lacked expression outside art class and may seem too intuitive and lacking in theory that would give educators something to teach and evaluate. Design's other face is technical and may be judged as too difficult and abstract for pre-college students. Again, computers and networking provide tools that can solve both problems.

Tools for Web authoring, image manipulation, drawing, and 3D rendering allow students to be creative and share their creations with others. There are meaningful concepts and skills students need to acquire in all areas of design that can be gained through the use of these tools.

On the techncial side, design and modelling tools can help students understand the technical ideas underlying design without having to master abstract mathematics or complex programming languages. Logo and its extensions—Boxer, StarLogo, NetLogo, and Microworlds—represent one important set of tools that make design education feasible at the precollege level. Logo has gotten a bad rap in education because it was ahead of its time. It was embraced by pioneers as THE answer to "computer literacy" and subsequently widely adopted for all the wrong reasons. The resulting backlash has left many educators with a persistent bad taste. This is unfortunate, because the Logo idea and the work of its inventors from MIT's Media Lab have articulated a new approach to education based on design.

Schools need to increase greatly their emphasis on teaching design. This will require fundamental structural changes in education. New goals will have to be articulated, standards articulated and courses developed. Profound learning happens when models student build to simulate reality meet data students collect. The combination of sophisticated data acquisition from probes and Internet databases with models that can be compared to data, can lead treakthroughs in learning. For example, "Kinetic Molecular Theory" is commonly taught in middle school science. The usual approach is to introduce a series of postulates roughly along the lines of "in an ideal gas, there are no attractive forces between molecules.

These molecules act as point particles that bounce off on another like pool balls without loosing energy." It is then asserted that these postulates predict the gas laws, but no justification is provided for this assertion. This must leave most students quite perplexed. First, the "ideal" gas is clearly incorrect; its molecules are not point particles, and there are forces between them. Students can change the size and forces between atoms and measure the resulting relationships between pressure, temperature, and volume.

The gas laws are obvious consequences this system, as is phase change, latent heat, and crystal structure. Using probes, the gas laws and latent heats predicted by the model can be quickly verified in real systems. Instead of the apparent complexity and inaccessibility of KMT as usually treated, this technology-rich approach clarifies the underlying concepts and relates the non-ideal properties of real liquids and solids to an ideal gas. The entire vocabulary of "ideal gases" and "KMT postulates", as well need to assert without proof that there is some relationship between the two, becomes unnecessary. The result is that students learn at a deeper level without encountering the confusion and apparent contradictions inherent in the usual approach.

Students had to wait that long for a fully satisfactory understanding. Even then, the formalism is so difficult, students often fail understand the science. Thus, educators at the precollege level have no choice but to present the material as facts that must be memorized and taken on faith. The combination of computer-based data collection and modelling can cause a breakthrough in student learning because it provides an alternative and more accessible way of understanding abstract concepts. Instead of using complex formal methods, a higher degree of student understanding can be gained by interacting with a suitable model. Deeper learning accessible to more students can be expected in all the sciences, mathematics, technical fields, quantitative social sciences, and business.

Genetics, macro-economics, chemical reactions, evolution, space shots, fire fighting, the stock market, global warming, epidemics, urban planning, and much more can be better understood through DOING it with a model than reading about it or trying to understand it through mathematics. The result will eventually be that many more abstract concepts will be taught at the pre-college level. This is essential to our economy because it is exactly these abstract ideas that fuel our economy. This breakthrough will have profound effects on special students.

For some, this will be liberating, for others, the increased emphasis on conceptual understanding will be make math and science even more baffling. The shift will probably catch many special educators napping who rely heavily on software for drill and practice. Since few special educators are strong in the concepts of science, math, and technology, becoming more concept-focused will put more pressure on classroom teachers to adapt to the needs of special students.

A major structural change will be needed to take advantage of modelling and data analysis tools. Teachers will be needed who have a deeper understanding of their subjects and who know how to teach these concepts with the appropriate use of educational technologies. Educators at all levels will have to adjust to the increased learning that is possible, including the test makers, standards setters, colleges, and schools of education. Unfortunately, tools have proven hard to use in education.

One form of this is "scaffolding", a variety of helping strategies that fade away as the user becomes more expert. Context-sensitive help, that annoying assistant-in-a-window in Microsoft Office, and tutorials are other strategies to address this problem. The alternative is to separate the tool from the pedagogical software. The tool should have no pedagogical strategy built into it. Instead, it should have "hooks" to a second software package we call Pedagogica. This is an application that is designed for controlling tools to achieve learning objectives. Pedagogica can control how many options the user sees, sense what users do with a tool, and interact directly with the user.

By changing the script that Pedagogica executes, it can provide help, scaffolding, or the full-featured tool. This means that the educational strategy is not determined by the tool and can be changed to adapt to the needs of the curriculum and students. One of the benefits of a tool like Pedagogica is that it can provide embedded assessment. The script that controls what material is presented to students needs to make judgements about what to present. This requires assessment of student learning that can be embedded in the tasks. For instance, consider the script that is used with a model of atoms in a box to teach that pressure and temperature are proportional under some conditions.

The script can observe whether a student has considered enough conditions to make this prediction. It can suggest new conditions and then observe what generalizations the student makes. Watching and guiding this kind of problem solving will give the software detailed data on what the student knows and can do. These data are essential for the software to provide useful guidance. It also provides invaluable assessment data.

The software can tell what a student has done, how long it took, how many blind alleys were pursued, and how persistent these errors were. We are building a graphical interface for Pedagogica in which the script closely resembles a concept map. This will allow educators to think in terms of concepts and understandings that are familiar and closely related to the mental models we hope student will develop.

Pedagogica is very much a work in progress, but something like this is needed to unleash the educational potential of general-purpose tools. We need to reach broad agreement on the need to separate pedagogy from tool applications and for the technical specifications of the "hooks" tools need to communicate with something like Pedagogica. Open source provides the best way to develop the needed educational tools. Open source software exists outside the normal commercial distribution channels, but supports commercialization and a flourishing service industry.

Businesses, from startups to IBM and Microsoft, surprisingly have learned to embrace open source. On the other hand, education has essentially ignored it. The only significant educational open source is a version of Logo by Brian Harvey and a productivity package, Star Office, that could see broad use in education. NSF sponsored research sometimes yields valuable educational software that is free during development, such as various versions of StarLogo, Image, and Biologica. Technically, these are not open source, since their developers retain the right to commercialize the software eventually. One of the reasons for the paucity of open source educational software is that the open source may need to be nurtured through enlightened self-interest.

Once there was a critical mass of open source system software it was in everyone's interest to expand that core.

If a hacker needed a Linux driver for an obscure printer, he or she would write it and be bound, under the terms of the GPL, to contribute it to the common good. There was also recognition from gurus for solid, well designed contributions. This suggests that educational open source could provide general-purpose languages, tools and simulations, especially if it was seeded with a critical mass and there were recognition for important contributions.

The critical difference between the current open source system and its possible application to education is the consumers. In the former case, the consumers are techies who can use the software with little or no assistance or ancillary information. In education, the consumers are nontechnical teachers and will need curriculum materials and professional development to use open source software. Perhaps this is not as large a distinction as it appears, however.

As the interest in open source has expanded, intermediaries have sprung up who consolidate and test open source software, provide documentation, and make it self-installing so that even nontechnical users can install it. Open source educational software is certain to receive increased interest as other countries begin to explore educational applications of technology. For instance, open source educational software is already beginning to make an impact in Mexico.

A university-based group had developed a graphical user interface for Linux and some applications that are being distributed free to all schools. Compared to the U.S., education in most other countries is more centralized, more closely connected to higher education, and far less likely to spend money on commercial software. As a result, there will be funding for software that will be distributed freely to schools. Since each country will have similar needs, it makes sense that software development be shared, and open source offers the best alternative. If funding is provided to seed and coordinate an international educational open source movement, we could unleash the kind of global creativity that has created and expanded open source software for business. The educational open source effort should concentrate on general-purpose tools with standardized hooks for pedagogical controllers like Pedagogica. If educational open source started this way, then enlightened self-interest could accelerate the process.

General-purpose tools could find worldwide application. Scripts would adapt the tools to the special needs and goals of specific countries and regions. If tools and scripts were open sourced, then every developer would have a powerful incentive to adhere to open source rules. There is certain to be thousands of bright, creative programmers throughout the world who would be thrilled to have the chance to contribute to improved education everywhere. The resulting educational tools and pedagogical scripts could be far more sophisticated and extensive than anything we can hope to develop through grants and business investment.

A coordinated effort to seed open source development could yield a rich harvest of educational applications that would be far better and broader than current software and completely free. This vision of learning that relies on tools guided by scripts using open source software leaves little room for traditional textbooks.

Current science texts for high school courses can exceed 1,000 pages and weigh more than a portable computer. They require, with associated materials, years and millions of dollars to develop. The texts must include every topic any significant sub-audience might want, while avoiding potential controversies. This huge investment results in high prices, the use of copyrighted content, and the inability to include public domain materials. This approach to curricula yields heavy, expensive books that are frozen in time. Even if they include software and Web pages, these ancillary materials only begin to scratch the surface of what is possible. They certainly fail to include sophisticated modelling and data collection tools.

The textbook-based approach to teaching science is too limiting and too inflexible; it belongs to the prior century. The realization of the power of technology requires a structural change in curriculum design and dissemination. The value of a textbook and its ancillary materials is that it represents a coherent aggregation of resources and educational activities.

Technology can provide the benefits of aggregation while avoiding the costs, inflexibility of a text and constraints of needing to own all the materials. This aggregation can be achieved through a flexible online curriculum framework with "slots" for modular digital materials that adhere to high standards. These slots might feature lab activities, software-based investigations, discussions of videos, structured investigations of a model, or research projects. The modules that fill the slots will come from sponsored educational R&D, academic researchers, teachers, or businesses. This modular structure would ensure far faster integration of materials originating in R&D labs that now often languish without a publisher. It is often incorrectly assumed that relying on digital materials isolates learners and deprives them from opportunities for direct, hands-on learning.

It is certainly possible and desirable to include in the curriculum collaboration and discussions both online and in-class and also give students ample opportunities to hands-on learning using probeware, off-line projects, activities, and field studies. A complete curriculum would consist of a framework with all slots filled with excellent, highly interactive, research-based materials that take full advantage of data and modelling tools. The result will be richer than a text, because it will provide interaction, computation, and collaboration in the context of learning resources.

A complete set of curriculum materials of this sort for a course might be produced with the same care as current texts, but be based on modules that can be easily modified or substituted for other materials as they become available. States and districts could modify the materials to fit their standards and interests. The modules requiring specialized labs, software, or technology could be modified to fit whatever a school has implemented. Some modules would be free, others would be licensed with a small fee in lieu of the textbook purchase costs, going to the authors.

Implementing these online curriculum resources will require that all students have easy access to computers and networking. This is, however, no reason to fail to start exploring this alternative to texts now. By the time high quality, fully integrated digital curriculum frameworks can be developed, filled, and tested, the technology will be ubiquitous. Tools, even with excellent pedagogical software, are not going to revolutionize education alone. These critical elements need to be integrated into courses students take. The process of changing courses can be excruciatingly slow.

Effective online courses are can accelerate this process by disseminating improved materials and techniques while also creating competition that can stimulate change. Effective courses are able to engage students at a distance in collaborative, activity-based learning, in small groups guided by trained facilitators. The best approaches use asynchronous, two-way technologies that rely on carefully designed activities, good evaluation strategies, and communities of learners facilitated by online discussions. They also take advantage of the computer for simulations, models, data collection, calculations, mentoring, and creations as appropriate.

Well-designed online courses are at least as good as face-to-face courses and are usually more inclusive and better designed. Only a fraction of the online courses fit these characteristics, but time will weed out the many poorer designs. Online courses for secondary students are exploding. At the advanced level, high school students can enroll at colleges and universities, one-third of which now offer Internet-based courses for credit.

Although slower than post-secondary education to exploit the power of online courses, high schools are increasingly offering effective online courses to their students. Secondary education has lagged colleges and universities in using online courses because few schools have the incentives or resources to offer courses themselves. Post-secondary institutions have strong financial incentives to increase income from tuitions from distant students.

High schools are chartered to serve a community and cannot increase their income by stealing students from other districts. In addition, post-secondary institutions tend to be larger and better able to afford the investment required to create effective online courses. The answer for secondary education is to form cooperatives of schools to share online courses. If each of 200 schools teaches a section of an online course, then all of their students have access to a pool of 200 course sections. Rather than competing for students in a zero-sum game, everyone gains from this form of sharing.

The costs are low, too, because schools in a cooperative don't have to pay tuition. If they balance out the number of seats they create through offering courses with the number of seats their students need, there are no new instructional costs. Of course, there are administrative costs in running the cooperative and training the participating staff, but these are less than tuition.

In US, the Department of Education's Technology Innovation Challenge program and resulted in the Virtual High School. Through four years of operation, we have demonstrated how such a cooperative can work. We have learned how to prepare teachers to offer online courses, how to keep standards high, and how to handle all the problems of scheduling, registration, orientation, and accreditation. The conclusion by independent evaluators from SRI International is that students, teachers, unions, and administrators love the VHS online courses. They are personal, challenging, and interesting. The courses offer quality, flexibility, and scope that is invaluable. Their range of topics is a godsend to students with specialized interests. Tiny schools can offer a range of courses that is the envy of larger schools not in the program.

At least two smaller schools were saved from oblivion because of this. The cooperative nature of the VHS is a key innovation that will prove essential in the long run. Some states, such as Florida and Kentucky, are beginning to offer online courses funded at the state level. These are doomed because they represent a major shift of instructional costs and control from the community to the state.

In the end, the states cannot afford this shift and communities and unions will not permit it. Similarly, for-profits or entrepreneurial colleges cannot expect to earn more than a tiny fraction of secondary school instructional costs because schools will want to keep those funds in the community. A larger district, however, should be able to sustain effective online courses in its high schools because it can act like a cooperative, sharing among schools instructional resources in the form of online courses. Once the idea of online courses takes off, it could force some much-needed change.

Advocates of vouchers and charter schools hope that the competition that their innovations introduce into education will provide incentives for all schools to improve. Cooperative online courses actually create a far more intense pressure to change, but without the competition. Once schools can offer hundreds of high quality online courses, parents and students will have little tolerance for substandard face-to-face courses. There will no excuse for courses that do not use technology well, that are not carefully designed, or are out-of-date. Students will protest with their feet and parents will demand access to the better online courses.

Online courses could be the quickest way to disseminate new instructional approaches that make full use of modelling and data tools. At first, these new approaches will attract only a fewstudents. The strength of online courses, however, is that they can reach thin audiences—those adventurous students willing to try a new approach. As data accumulates about the power of these alternatives, there will be demand for additional sections.

The creation of educational cooperatives is an example the kind of structural shifts that are needed to exploit the information technologies. To exploit the power of online course, it is not sufficient simply to offer some courses. A set of economic, political, and practical problems must be solved which seem to demand cooperative sharing of courses. Effective online courses can revolutionize teacher professional development (TPD). They are able to deliver focused and timely assistance to teachers whenever they need it.

Online teacher professional development during the academic year allows teachers to experiment with the new materials and approaches advocated in a course and then discuss the results with their colleagues. Inherently, the costs for effective online TPD are lower than face-to-face courses and workshops because they avoid transportation, food, and meeting expenses. One of the most exciting current developments in TPD is the use of online interactive video case studies in online courses.

The technology is nearing the capacity to handle video on demand, at least in short segments. This allows to imagine that large numbers of videos of exemplary teaching could be made widely available. It is well known that video case studies, properly supported, are far more effective for teacher than hours of abstract discussions or readings of how to teach. A video shows an entire environment, illustrates how to organize classroom space and time, and how respond to students' typical issues. The rapid changes in standards, assessment, content, curricula, and educational technologies create a massive need for ongoing teacher professional development.

Technology itself puts new burdens on teachers. It is increasingly clear that every school will have a unique and rapidly changing combination of computers, networking, and software. Teachers cannot rely on textbooks to provide software and network resources coordinated with the text because they cannot be sure what technology will be available.

Consequently, the task of integrating technology is left to teachers. Teachers need detailed and specific help in adapting to these changes and new responsibilities. Online courses, on the other hand, can reach thin markets with excellent courses designed by the best people in the field. While enough teachers to make up a workshop from one school are unlikely to need the same highly focused course, it is likely that a critical number can be found across the country on almost any conceivable topic.

Many teachers who are enthusiastic about online courses and praise them for what they have learned, fail to complete their courses. One exception has been the courses we offer in the VHS that are a prerequisite to teaching in the VHS. Here, unlike many TPD situations, successful completion is an absolute requirement for continuing in the project.

The problem is that teachers are incredibly busy and are seldom given released time for online TPD. In addition, there are seldom strong incentives for completion. The upshot is that even conscientious teachers tend to stay enrolled just long enough to get the materials and main ideas and then leave. This means that online courses should be short and highly focused and that successful completion should well rewarded. Teachers should be able to select exactly the content they need and be able to absorb it in minimal time. What is needed, then, is the development of very large numbers of targeted online short courses for teachers that make liberal use of video case studies.

These should be a half-semester long and accredited by a rigorous, external body. Schools need to expect their teachers continually to complete short courses that fit into the school's master plan for TPD, provide released time for the courses, and link advancement to successful completion. Designing and offering courses online requires skill, knowledge, and discipline. The reason there are so many poor online courses is that teachers and entrepreneurs assume that this is an easy task for any teacher.

To fill the need for disseminating the knowledge we have gained, we created "metacourses", online courses about online courses. For instance, in the VHS course we have developed two that are central to the success of the project. The first is a yearlong 125 hour course about designing, creating, and offering a VHS course. The second is a one-semester course on how to offer an online course. As part of a different project, we have developed "Moving Out of the Middle", a popular course on facilitating online courses. The nation needs many more secondary teachers trained in online courses. If we can get to college students who are making career choices, the opportunity to teach online might help attract more well qualified students into teaching. Being able to teach online can solve the problems of two jobs for married students.

The ability of one spouse to teach online vastly simplifies the choice of location and opens more options for the other spouse. In addition, online teaching is likely to be well paying because the online teacher can accept the best job anywhere. The opportunity to earn more and telecommute anywhere might be deciding factors for attracting outstanding students interested in teaching but discouraged by pay and working conditions.

Schools of education and licensing agencies will have to agree that online teaching is realistic option for students and that there are important things to learn about online teaching. This is likely to take decades without a concerted research and development effort. In short, schools need to undertake major changes to fully exploit technology. Students will need increased access to technology. This will make it feasible to rely more on tool-type applications.

Realizing the potential gains in learning will greatly strain schools. Teachers will need increased professional development in both content and the use of technology. Online courses will provide models for how to do this along with new opportunities for professional development. Online courses will also provide the spur of competition. Students and parents will demand face-to-face courses of the same quality available online. If schools cannot meet that demand, they will loose students to home schooling or alternative schools better able to exploit the technology.

Funding agencies could greatly accelerate the changes needed to realize these dreams. Small studies are needed to find out what technology-enhanced learning is possible under ideal conditions. Large-scale, longitudinal experiments are need to work out the bugs and document the gains in student learning that are possible. Funding should be provided to develop and disseminate the needed online professional development and the training of online facilitators through metacourses.

The development of high-performance computing and communications is creating new media, such as the World Wide Web and virtual reality. In turn, these new media enable new types of messages and experiences; for example, interpersonal interactions in immersive, synthetic environments lead to the formation of virtual communities.

The innovative kinds of pedagogy empowered by these emerging media, messages, and experiences make possible a transformation of conventional distance education—which replicates traditional classroom teaching across barriers of distance and time—into an alternative instructional paradigm: distributed learning. What does the evolution of new media mean for distance educators? A medium is in part a channel for conveying content; new media such as the internet allow us to readily reach wider, more diverse audiences.

Just as important, however, is that a medium is a representational container enabling new types of messages (e.g., a picture is worth a thousand words). Because the process of thinking is based on representations like language and imagery, the process of learning is strongly shaped by the types of instructional messages we can exchange with students. Emerging representational containers like hypermedia enable a broader, more powerful repertoire of pedagogical strategies. The global marketplace and the communications and entertainment industries are driving the rapid evolution of high-performance computing and communications.

Regional, national, and global information infrastructures are being developed to enhance our abilities to sense, act, and learn across barriers of distance and time. The ways in which information is created, delivered, and used in business, government, and society are swiftly changing. To successfully prepare students as workers and citizens, educators must incorporate experiences creating and utilising new forms of expression, such as multimedia, in the curriculum.

Information infrastructures offer channels for delivering these technology-intensive learning experiences to any place on demand. The information superhighway metaphor now widely used to convey the implications of high-performance computing and communications is inadequate. Such an analogy is the equivalent of someone in 1896 declaring that the airplane will be the canal system of the 20th century. Backward-looking metaphors focus on what we can automate—how we can use channels to send conventional forms of content more efficiently—but they miss the true innovation: redefining how we communicate and educate by using new types of messages and experiences to be more effective.

Because emerging forms of representation such as hypermedia and virtual reality are in the early stages of development, we are just beginning to understand how they shape not only their messages but their users. Many people are still reeling from the first impact of high-performance computing and communications—shifting from the challenge of not getting enough information to the challenge of surviving too much information.

The core skill for today's workplace is not foraging for data but filtering a plethora of incoming information. The emerging literacy we all must master requires diving into a sea of information and immersing ourselves in data in order to harvest patterns of knowledge, just as fish extract oxygen from water with their gills. As educators, understanding how to structure learning experiences to make such immersion possible is the core of the new rhetoric.

Expanding traditional definitions of literacy and rhetoric into immersion-centered experiences of interacting with information is crucial to preparing students for full participation in 21st-century society. Conventional distance education is similar to traditional classroom instruction except that it uses technology-based delivery systems.

In contrast, emerging forms of distributed learning are leading to a reconceptualisation of education's mission, clients, process, and content. This new instructional paradigm is based on shifts in what learners need to be prepared for the future as well as on new capabilities in the pedagogical repertoire of teachers. Using information infrastructures, educators and students can join distributed conferences that provide an instant network of contacts who have useful skills and immediate answers to questions.

In time, these informal sources of expertise will utilise embedded groupware tools to enhance collaboration. On the internet, online archival resources are increasingly linked to the World Wide Web, accessible through webcrawlers like Mosaic and Netscape. Eventually, artificial-intelligence-based guides will facilitate navigating through huge amounts of stored information.

Virtual exhibits that duplicate real-world settings (e.g., museums) are emerging; these environments make a wide variety of experiences possible without the necessity of travel or scheduling. Distributed science projects enable shared experiments to be conducted across time and space, with each team member learning more about the phenomenon being studied and about scientific investigation than would be possible in isolation. Combined, all these capabilities to enhance information-gathering and creation form knowledge webs.

However, access to data does not automatically expand students' knowledge; the availability of information does not intrinsically create an internal framework of ideas that learners can use to interpret reality. Although presentational approaches transmit material rapidly from source to student, this content often evaporates quickly from learners' minds. To be motivated to master concepts and skills, students need to see the connection between what they are learning and the rest of their lives and the mental models they already use.

Even when learners are drilled in a topic until facts are indefinitely retained—we all know that the sum of a triangle's internal angles is 180 degrees—this knowledge is often "inert;" most people don't know how to apply the abstract principles they memorised in school to real-world problems. To move students from assimilating inert facts into generating mental models, teachers must structure learning experiences that highlight how new ideas can provide insights in intriguing and challenging situations. The curriculum is already overcrowded with low-level information; teachers frantically race through required material, helping students memorise factual data to be regurgitated on mandated, standardised tests.

Using information infrastructures as a fire hose to spray more information into educational settings would make this situation even worse. Without skilled facilitation, many learners who access current knowledge webs will flounder in a morass of unstructured data. A vital, emerging form of literacy that educators must communicate is how to transform archival information into personal knowledge.

However, moving students from access through assimilation to appropriation requires educational experiences that empower knowledge construction by unsophisticated learners, helping them make sense of massive, incomplete, and inconsistent information sources.

Modular Technology Education Programme (MTE)

MTE is generally thought of as a curriculum provided by a commercial vendor in which students learn about an area of technology by:

- participating in interactive media presentations,
- following instructions in workbooks,
- writing responses in student journals, and
- experimenting and building projects.

Many MTE curricula have a strong "hands-on" component in which students use tools to process resources, generally resulting in a completed prototype or experiment. Personal computers are replacing the classroom teacher as the disseminator of technological content and processes in modular programs. The modular approach is relatively new to our profession and largely untested as to its instructional efficacy.

Furthermore, MTE is replacing traditional technology education programs at an unprecedented rate. In an effort to determine the prevalence of MTE programs in America's public schools, the following strategies were pursued: a) the main MTE companies, in terms of market share, were contacted relative to numbers of installed labs, b) data were compiled relative to secondary school counts, and c) percentage frequencies were calculated for middle and high school MTE facilities. Representatives from eight companies were contacted.

An MTE lab consists of eight or more modular work stations with a computerised management system. Six of the eight companies contacted were willing to reveal the number of MTE labs that they have installed as of September 2001. Among the six responding companies, there were 5,088 middle-level and 2,177 high school MTE labs. The researcher has determined the existence of 17,542 public middle/ intermediate schools in America and 15,391 high schools.

Middle/intermediate school numbers were compiled by adding secondary school counts by states in Patterson's American Education 2000 edition data for grades 5-9, 7-12, and K-12. Data for high schools were compiled by adding data for grades 7-12, 9-12, 10-12, and

K-12. Dividing 5,088 by 17,542 indicates that 29% of American middle/intermediate school contain a modular program. Similarly, dividing 2,177 by 15,391 indicates that 14% of American high schools have modular programs.

These MTE frequency data are conservative estimates since only about three-quarters of the major MTE companies provided data and because both 7-12 and K-12 schools were used in calculating both middle/intermediate frequency and high school frequency numbers. These data support the widespread adoption of MTE across the US. Through observation and teaching experience in a modular lab, the researcher has observed variance in students' ability to master the learning tasks presented via the computer-assisted instruction (CAI) used in MTE.

Some students excel in modular programs while others struggle. As the modular approach replaces traditional technology education programs, questions arise concerning how students' individual traits and characteristics interact with the learning tasks presented in this instructional paradigm. Limited research has been conducted regarding these relationships. Traditionally, schools emphasise the use of externally supplied rewards and punishments as a means of controlling behavior and in directing the learning process.

Modular programs, however, require a shift away from external motivation strategies in which students are rewarded and punished by the teacher. MTE programs, with their self-paced CAI instructional approach, require students to be intrinsically motivated. MTE posttest scores from a unit on engineering structures taught by CAI. Continuous (i.e., interval level) data were collected with a fifty point MTE posttest instrument developed by the researcher.

Cognitive style of the subjects was determined through the Group Embedded Figures Test (GEFT). The motivation of the subjects was determined through the Children's Academic Intrinsic Motivation Instrument (CAIMI). The CAI multimedia presentations consisted of narrated text, music, sound effects, video animations, photographs, and hypertext links. Activities started with directions presented on the computer monitor.

Consistent with the instructional design of the module, dyads navigated the multimedia presentations at their own rate. The computer program used to presented several multimedia selections. Subjects were stopped by the CAI program to answer questions in an electronic journal. The CAI program summarised the material presented in each lesson. The researcher observed that many subjects were not following the CAI program in the proper instructional order and appeared to be confused. The magnitude of the relationships between students' posttest scores with verbal ability and prior knowledge was surprising.

As bivariate predictors, verbal ability accounted for 53.5% and prior knowledge 55.1% of the total MTE posttest variance in this sample. Multiple regression was used in the multivariate analysis to determine the existence of relationships between MTE posttest scores (dependent variable) and the students' cognitive style, verbal ability, quantitative ability, and intrinsic motivation (independent variables). Based upon the bivariate analysis, it is reasonable to conclude that verbal ability and prior knowledge enable a student to do better on the MTE posttest. Quantitative ability, cognitive style, and intrinsic motivation correlated significantly with MTE posttest scores in the bivariate analysis. However, these variables "washed out" in the multivariate analysis.

The predictor variables used in the multivariate analysis did not show multicollinearity with each other. CAIMI displayed a low correlation with MTE posttest scores in the bivariate analysis. The CAIMI variable may not have been an accurate measurement of the intrinsic motivation construct. The multiple regression model developed to determine whether students were at risk in terms of MTE achievement. A profile for low achieving students was developed in this analysis; the identification and remediation of "MTE low-achievers" was one objective of this research project.

Finnish technology education, called "technical work" in the national curriculum guidelines, is a school subject in which pupils design and make products by using different materials, machines, processes, techniques and tools. This emphasis on designing and making is an essential part of Finnish technology education. It is believed that such experiences develop pupils' knowledge, personal qualities, and psychomotor skills.

As with the traditional (sloyd) programs that preceded it, there is general belief that the design and build approach used in contemporary technology education programs enhances the pupils' creativity, dexterity, diligence, initiative, problem solving, self-image, and preparation for work. As technology education has evolved in Finland, more content has been introduced, including such areas as electricity, electronics, machinery, and computers.

Construction kits for teaching control technology have also been adopted. In addition, technology education classes now offers pupils the opportunity to service and repair their bicycles, mopeds, and other technical equipment. These areas, combined with the more traditional sloyd (craft and design), have made Finnish technology education more diverse than in other Scandinavian countries. In informal discussions among teachers and teacher educators, there seems to be a general feeling that technology education in Finnish primary schools is out of date, emphasising older technological processes such as the making of wooden and metal items.

Even though technology education has been updated to an extent, there is a general feeling that there should be more connection to the modern technological world than that which exists presently. The technological concepts of communication, construction, energy, manufacturing, and transportation are rarely reviewed from ecological, economical, cultural, and social viewpoints.

The activities in which the pupils are engaged determine the kinds of technological knowledge and processes they learn. These activities must therefore be upgraded. The Finnish comprehensive school provides compulsory basic education to pupils between the ages of 7 and 16. It is divided into a six-year lower level (grades 1-6), which corresponds internationally to primary education, and a three-year upper stage (grades 7-9), corresponding to lower secondary education. In the third grade of the primary school, it is compulsory that all pupils study technology education.

After that they have to choose either technology education or textile work. As one might expect, boys usually choose the former and girls choose the latter.

Pupils who have chosen technology education study it for at least two hours a week from third through sixth grades.

In Finnish primary schools, technology education is usually taught by regular classroom teachers. Today these teachers must hold a master's degree in education and most have studied technology education as part of their teacher preparation program. A separate technology education room is provided for instruction, with an ideal maximum of 16 students in the facility at one a time. The national curriculum reform in 1994 gave schools noticeably more freedom in developing their own curricula.

The national core curriculum and curricular guidelines are very vague, providing only brief outlines. Though this allows for local flexibility, it also increases the diversity in the way in which technology education is taught from one school to another. In the latest national core curriculum, the main emphasis is on the "idea-to-product" process, with the pupil fully engaged in designing.

Although, the designing and making of products remains as the central part of the national curriculum guidelines, the need for a broader technological understanding and capability is also mentioned. The Finnish curriculum guidelines mention creativity, cultural heritage, environmental education, entrepreneur education, self-image, problem solving skills, social skills, and readiness for work life as the general goals of a comprehensive education.

The responding teachers were asked to describe the extent to which pupils' activities in technology education corresponded to the goals. Technology education focuses most on students' creativity. The development of problem-solving skills, self-image, cultural heritage, and social skills are also often associated with technology education.

However, readiness for work life, environmental education, and entrepreneur education are associated to only a limited extent with technology education according to the responding teachers. Traditional product design-based work includes the development of manual dexterity, product planning, work safety, work education, and aesthetic education. The results indicated that manual dexterity was most central to the product design-based work.

In addition, work education, work safety, and product planning were considered essential components. Aesthetics were considered to be a limited part of teaching and the pupils' work. It also included an assessment of the three dimensions of technological literacy as espoused by Dyrenfurth and Kozak and others: the utilisation of technology, the evaluation of technology, and the appreciation of technology. The utilisation of technology refers to the acquisition of the knowledge and skills necessary to use and make technological products and solutions.

The evaluation of technology refers to the critical evaluation of the impact and consequences of technological processes. The appreciation of technology refers to understanding the outcomes of technological innovations as they relate to a higher standard of living. One approach used in technology education involves students in the making of artifacts using prescribed drawings or plans. Pupils can also invent, design and make products by themselves. This second method is referred to as the "design teaching method." The lack of financial resources determines what type of teaching materials may be purchased. In turn, this relates to the teachers' perceptions about delivering a valid technology education program.

The lack of financial resources was followed by the lack of teaching ideas and the lack of other accompanying resources. The latter is related to classroom tools, machines, and other equipment that must be purchased with resources other than those used for supplies and materials. No significant differences among the respondents were found for the top three obstacles listed above. Though not at the top of the list, motivation was one of the obstacles identified. It was found that older teachers felt that they had significantly less motivation compared to younger teachers. In short, the aim in developing technology education in primary schools is not to create a technology education classroom wherein pupils only read textbooks, watch videos, use computer software, and complete worksheets.

The cultural, economic, natural, and social aspects, together with the technological aspects, should be considered in connection with designing and making products. Chemical and biotechnology could also be taught in conjunction with science, although they can also be taught in connection with design and making processes. The history of technology could be correlated to humanities classes as well. In summary, the objects designed and made in technology education should not be "museum artifacts," but rather ones that are relevant to modern society. An example of such a project might be an electronic device found in some modern consumer product.

In designing and making products, pupils should be taught to reflect upon the impact and consequences of technology to the society and the environment around them.

The concept of technical education in New Zealand as it developed from the British model. It examines how England and Wales designed and introduced a new technology curriculum, and how, of necessity, a New Zealand technology curriculum has been developed which is more suited to New Zealand's developing culture.

It illustrates some of the good features and some of the difficulties resulting from the introduction of technology as a subject in New Zealand schools in 1999. The educational system of New Zealand, a former British colony, has understandably been influenced by the British school system. The public primary schooling system introduced in 1877 was made freely available to as many children as possible, and was "modelled on British and Australian counterparts".

The late 19th century introduction of secondary schools to New Zealand was unashamedly academic. The secondary schools aligned themselves with the University of New Zealand by adopting the Matriculation Examination as an entrance requirement to University.

According to Lee, "English thinking dominated schooling policy and practice in the young colony...secondary schools were inaccessible to most youth, particularly working class children". In 1901 a free place system was introduced in which every child was to be offered a free place in a secondary school. The tendency that followed was for most pupils to remain at secondary school for a short period only, while following an academic course. The Minister of Lands in 1900 stated, "it was obviously the case in that children in the rural areas should be studying technical or agriculture subjects that would have a distinct bearing on the occupations in those localities". As a result, by 1910 technical high schools had been established in the major centres throughout the country.

This secondary school system now simulated the British tradition where middle class and academically strong went to a public or grammar school, and the working class went to a technical high school. As a typical example of this division in the early secondary education, the city of Hamilton is a small inland New Zealand city at the centre of one of the richest agricultural and pastoral areas in the world. Hamilton had two secondary schools until the late 1950's, and prospective students were required take an entrance exam as a requirement to gain entry to Hamilton High School (HHS).

The remaining students went to the Hamilton Technical College (HTC) for a technical (or pre-vocational) education. The Hamilton historian Gibbons described HTC as offering practical instruction for quite specific skills and careers, "to teach practical knowledge to the artisans and labourers of the future". New Zealand's technical high schools typically offered boys pre-vocational streams of engineering, building, or an agricultural course to give them a practical skill preparing them for the nonprofessional workforce. Academically less able female students were offered a commerce stream with subjects like typing and bookkeeping to prepare them for commerce, where it was expected that they would work, or alternatively as Gibbons described, "needlework, cooking and domestic economy".

The small populations of the rural districts could not sustain a two-school system, and these post-primary schools, of necessity, continued to be mixed or comprehensive. Such a system in these schools was now similar to the early British secondary school system on which ours was modelled. As described by Black "the major subject had hitherto been academic, with the vocational studies reserved for older students classed as less academically able". De Vries described a similar system in the Netherlands in which the courses were categorised as either "pre-vocational or pre-university". The technical high school system, (or the technical streams in the comprehensive school), offered the students an education that they would otherwise perhaps not get.

In Newzealand, the Technical high school system had some drawbacks: Although a technical education was commonly thought to give the students who left school at the age of fifteen a useful start in industry, commerce, farming, or homemaking, it became increasingly so at the expense of a more rounded general and intellectual education.

Within the British origin of a class system, this was never a concern in the British education system on which it was modelled. Pre-vocational courses were generally perceived (by parents and students) as for less able students, giving the subjects a low status, even if this was never the intention of a particular school offering the subjects.

McKenzie observed "Inherited attitudes of the United Kingdom were an added handicap. In Britain, separate technical schools were typically associated in the public mind with second class knowledge which provided the limited skills and disciplined work habits of a docile working class". Similarly, the common fear of ambitious youth in New Zealand was that if they were directed into technical curricula, their vocational opportunities would be restricted. The system was sexist.

The provision of a vocationally oriented education in reality, as O'Neil subtly put it, "meant the formalised entrenchment of gender differentiated (practical) vocational courses...male pupils took vocational courses for their future paid employment, some females took them for theirs, but many did so in the light of their expected future in unpaid domestic labour". By the 1930s, there was a strong case to dispense with the two types of school, and thereby dispense with the associated class attitudes.

In 1945 the Department of Education imposed a common core curriculum on all types of schools. This did not inhibit the ambitions of the academics or frustrate the aspirations of the ambitious, but it ensured a common range of studies, including craft subjects for the junior pupils. Students at post primary schools were able to take technical subjects, including workshop craft subjects.

While this education system and its crafts may have been appropriate for earlier times, in more recent years it has generated some problems. Frequently, the technology learned in schools did not help students in society because the equipment they used was often industrial or commercial cast-off and therefore likely to be obsolete and out-of-date. The school environment can be unrealistic and lack an examination of the social issues of technology. There is nothing wrong with craft skills themselves as an element in education.

The problem with traditional craft teaching‹woodwork, for example‹as an educational endeavour has rather been that the disciplines are learned within a context that limits their general applicability to build a coffee table in school is to learn not a generalised competence capable of application anywhere but a competence for one context, school. The teaching of technical subjects requires skilled teaching staff. The separate technical and craft learning activities in New Zealand tended to be isolated from each other.

The technological knowledge areas were not linked in a structured manner in which the knowledge could transfer from one situation to another. The curriculum did not encourage team working. In today's work environment it is likely that a professional will have to work in a group relationship to solve a problem or operate a system. ral individuals whose work must be coordinated". The curriculum was not considered responsive to New Zealand's particular needs, languages, and cultural differences.

Although New Zealand has this long history of technical education in the intermediate and secondary schools, the delivery of general secondary school education has not always related the students to a realistic social framework of knowledge which is applicable to an increasingly technological world. What is required is a technical education system for all students.

However, unlike the traditional technology programs, which formerly taught only skill-based programs, the technology instruction in schools must change to meet the needs of a technologically advanced society. New Zealand underwent major curriculum reforms in the 1990's The development of a national curriculum was part of this reform. This resulted from growing concerns with school curriculum. During the 1970s and 1980s, calls were made for a curriculum that was responsive to New Zealand's needs for people highly skilled in science and technology, and with the language and cultural sensitivity needed to maintain international economic competitiveness.

Technology subjects need to be accessible to all children, regardless of gender or social standing. Along this line, Black and Harrison proffered the general idea of technological capability with a task-action-capability (TAC) approach. The Government of New Zealand undertook a revision of curriculum in 1990 under the banner of *The Achievement Initiative*. The object was to explore ideas influenced by the curriculum reforms that were taking place in England and Wales. A Ministerial Task Group Reviewing Science and Technology Education was set up in 1991 which made many recommendations, the most significant being that a technology curriculum be developed as an area in its own right.

The New Zealand technology curriculum is the result of a group of experienced curriculum writers, some of whom had experience in rewriting the science and mathematics curriculums. The development policy was a result of the wider community input and also a result of much international research into technical education, teaching, and learning. The New Zealand curriculum is not simply the copy of an overseas model with a few wording changes. It is a break from the British modelling of the past, with a new subject that is reflective of New Zealand conditions and culture, and with a knowledge base of its own which incorporates a balance of intellectual, social, and personal interactions with technology.

The curriculum appears to be well balanced. It is not a fragmented assemblage that tries to cobble together a whole spectrum of existing subjects and crafts. The design may be varied to suit particular areas of the country and it is also versatile enough to reflect current technological practices. It may be difficult for the technology curriculum to succeed until it has full status, equal to other subjects in the school curriculum.

The former areas of arts and crafts that were rather specialised are now merged into a new curriculum where technology teachers are no longer required to be expert in a very narrow field of technology. Most of the nontechnical teachers will initially lack the appropriate technological expertise.

Similarly, the former specialised subject teachers will now require more general knowledge and skills in technology and education. The recommendation of the Ministry of Research, Science, and Technology to provide for adequate training and resourcing must be taken very seriously. It follows from the above that the teachers will not always have the answers and must of necessity change their roles to mentors and facilitators. While the successful teaching of the subject will encourage talking, the exchange of ideas, questioning, and curiosity which is excellent for the development of group dynamics, some children's cultures do not encourage it.

The standard New Zealand primary classrooms do not have facilities to out carry some of the curriculum projects. The development and implementation of the subject can easily be undermined by misinterpretation. To solve these problems, and successfully implement the technology curriculum, the teaching of technology as we have known it in the past will change. Vincent and Vincent stated that "curriculum change may denote bringing about changes in methods of teaching and learning, as well as changes in the programmes or courses".

The curriculum states that a timetable for the subject of technology "allows for teachers to work collaboratively in planning and delivery". Effective planning of the subject necessitates an increase in the number of meetings the teachers must attend which, in turn, has increased their workload. Recognition of this problem has resulted in a reduced requirement for teaching technology in the first year of the programme[1]s implementation. Technological knowledge is increasing at an exponential rate and the professionals of today work in environments where they can no longer be expected to learn in advance all the technological knowledge required to solve day-to-day problems.

Knowledge must constantly be acquired in order to understand technology and solve the problems of the time. It is difficult to train a person for a professional situation where the demands of tasks may be to some extent unpredictable, and where the knowledge and skills needed are not usually defined by some prior instruction or coaching of the concept or process.

McCormick stated: "Technological activity is by nature multidimensional, requiring understanding from a variety of points of view". In addition, most people working in a technological occupation must retrain in technology at least once in their working lifetime.

As this knowledge explosion continues, the balance between *what to learn* and *how to learn* must shift towards the latter. Given the impossibility of knowing everything about anything, the educational requirements for a job and those for higher education are converging. The Carnegie Task Force observed that "...the economic and social needs of our country will force us to provide for many the kind of education previously reserved for the elite few". New Zealand education has taken positive steps to define and establish technology education as an academic discipline to replace traditional school craft subjects. All students are expected to study technology following a structured progression of the curriculum from their first year in primary school to their senior secondary year 13.

The success of the technology curriculum will depend upon its successful implementation in the schools, together with the development of an effective assessment program. Naturally it will take time to develop a culture of technology education in New Zealand schools, as "...technology education does not have a historical home in New Zealand".

The exams that students sit in the 7th form (the final secondary school year required as a university entrance qualification) are the exams that possess social status. It can be expected that the subject of technology will gain an appropriate social status and break its current shackles as a pre-vocational course when it eventually becomes a 7th Form exam. The examination unit standards for the subject are currently being written and will be phased in gradually, starting in 2001.

A panel of academic professionals is developing the achievement standards, professional development requirements, and resources for year eleven and will be introduced in 2000. Unlike the old pre-vocation training in the technical schools, the new subject of technology will be of assistance in acquainting the New Zealand pupils with the aspects of technology that are important in the 21st century. It will provide students with the knowledge and skills that will be useful, regardless of the career path they choose, by increasing their options, horizons, and perspectives).

The process that resulted in Technology in the New Zealand Curriculum was designed to give the students an understanding of the culture, the values, and the social issues involved with technology. It is intended to bring the concept of technological literacy into the intellectual domain.

Such an understanding and intellectual approach to technology is now deemed necessary for all students in order for them to function effectively in our modern technological society.

The new subject will lay a good foundation for further technological learning in school as well as the inevitable learning that takes place outside the school in the home and at work. Nickerson went even further in expressing the view that technology education will "...increase one's appreciation of other cultures, viewpoints and lifestyles, and deepen one's sensitivities to other people's rights, feelings, preferences and hopes...it should heighten one's curiosity and inquisitiveness; as a consequence of one[1]s education, the world should be a far more interesting place than it would otherwise be".

Productivity in Technology Education

A creative product is one that possesses some degree of unusualness (originality) and usefulness. When given the opportunity for self-expression, a student's project becomes nothing less than a creative product. The creative product can be viewed as a physical representation of a person's "true" creative ability encapsulating both the creative person and process.

By examining the literature related to the creative person and process, technology educators may gain a deeper understanding of the creative product itself. Inventors such as Edison and Ford have been recognised as being highly creative. Why some people reach a level of creative genius while others do not is still unknown.

However, Maslow, after studying several of his subjects, determined that all people are creative, not in the sense of creating great works, but rather, creative in a universal sense that attributes a portion of creative talent to every person. In trying to understand and predict a person's creative ability, two factors have often been considered: intelligence and personality. Researchers have shown that there are certain personality traits associated with creative people. Runco, Nemiro, and Walberg identified and conducted a survey investigating personality traits associated with the creative person.

The survey was mailed to 400 individuals who had submitted papers and/or published articles related to creativity. The researchers asked participants to rate, in order of importance, various traits that they believed affected creative achievement. The survey contained 16 creative achievement clusters consisting of 141 items. One hundred and forty-three surveys were returned reflecting a response of 35.8%. Results demonstrated that intrinsic motivation, problem finding, and questioning skills were considered the most important traits in predicting and identifying creative achievement.

Though personality traits play an important part in understanding creative ability, an equally important area of creativity theory lies in the identification of the creative process itself. Creativity is a process that has been represented using various models. Wallas offered one of the earliest explanations of the creative process.

Wallas' model has served as a foundation upon which other models have been built. Some researchers have added the communication stage to the creative process. The communication stage is the final stage of the creative process.

At this stage, the new idea confined to one's mind is transformed into a verbal or nonverbal product. The product is then shared within a social context in order that others may react to and possibly accept or reject it. A more comprehensive description of the creative process is captured within a definition offered by Torrance.

Creativity is a process of becoming sensitive to problems, deficiencies, gaps in knowledge, missing elements, disharmonies, and so on; identifying the difficult; searching for solutions, making guesses or formulating hypotheses about the deficiencies, testing and re-testing these hypotheses and possibly modifying and re-testing them, and finally communicating the results.

Torrance's definition resembles what some have referred to as problem solving. For example, technology educators Savage and Sterry, generalising from the work of several scholars, identified six steps to the problem-solving process:

— *Defining the problem*: Analysing, gathering information, and establishing limitations that will isolate and identify the need or opportunity.

— *Developing alternative solutions*: Using principles, ideation, and brainstorming to develop alternate ways to meet the opportunity or solve the problem.

— *Selecting a solution*: Selecting the most plausible solution by identifying, modifying, and/or combining ideas from the group of possible solutions.

— *Implementing and evaluating the solution*: Modelling, operating, and assessing the effectiveness of the selected solution.

— *Redesigning the solution*: Incorporating improvements into the design of the solution that address needs identified during the evaluation phase.

— *Interpreting the solution*: Synthesising and communicating the characteristics and operating parameters of the solution.

Creative problem solving is a subset of problem- solving based on the assumption that not all problems require a creative solution. He surmised that when a problem is solved with a learned response, then no creativity has been expressed.

However, when a simple problem is solved with an insightful response, then a small measure of creativity has been expressed, when a complex problem is solved with a novel solution, then genuine creativity has occurred. Genuine creativity is the result of the creative process that manifests itself into a creative product. Understanding the creative process as well as the creative person may play an important role in realising the true nature of the creative product.

Though researchers have not reached a consensus as to what attributes make up the creative product, identifying and evaluating the creative product has been a concern of some researchers. Moss and Duenk have arguably conducted the most extensive research establishing criteria for evaluating creative products within industrial arts/technology education. Moss, in examining the criterion problem, concluded that unusualness (originality) and usefulness were the defining characteristics of the creative product produced by industrial arts students.

4

Technology Integration Education

A focus on change at the school and system level is integrated into the program through the seminar topics and through an on-line mentoring process. In US, a small, but important feature of the York Principals' Qualification Program (PQP) is taught via computer-mediated communication to groups of candidates who converse on-line.

In contrast to the course seminars, the on-line groups are not site-based. PQP candidates are randomly assigned to online discussion groups. Each on-line group consists of 15 - 20 candidates who are mentored by two principals from different Boards of Education in the GTA. The On-Line Mentors are volunteers and represent a variety of Public and Catholic Boards.

They are recruited for their knowledge and experience, and for their 'fit' with the underlying principles of the York PQP. Each week, the On-Line Mentors post cases for discussion drawn from their everyday experiences as principals. The on-line component of the program was developed for a number of reasons:

a) To provide the opportunity for ongoing learning using computer-mediated technologies, including electronic mail and Internet information resources.

b) To broaden the candidates knowledge of the range of issues and administrative practices of different Boards of Education across the GTA, for example to highlight differences between rural and urban schools, mono-cultural and multi-cultural schools, schools that are monolingual and those with a broad linguistic diversity.

c) To extend the range of contacts so useful to recently appointed administrators.

d) To provide a different learning medium for the candidates—one that is non-linear, reflective, and not tied to the schedules of face-to-face teaching and learning.

Indeed, the on-line technology allows for networking across the large distances of the GTA, and provides the opportunity for people working in diverse school situations to learn from each other through the discussion of cases drawn from the everyday experience of principals working across the diversity of GTA schools. Case methodology has a long history in education for leadership and administration.

It originated as an instructional technique at Harvard University Law School in 1870 and later became widely accepted in a variety of professional disciplines. A case as an account or description of a situation or sequence of events confronting an individual, a group of individuals, or an organization. Rather than deliver concepts and theories, cases (also called clinical correlation, leadership stories, real-life narratives, critical incidents, and vignettes) present situations for analysis about which decisions must be made.

There are similarities of structure between case histories, clinical cases, problem-based learning and other experientially based methods in that they are all oriented to the particularities of practice while drawing on the generalities of theory. The purpose of cases and case-based instruction in any professional field relates directly to the nature of the body of knowledge that exists in that particular field.

For example, in teacher education cases are used to develop reflective practitioners and to promote teacher reflection and enhanced understanding. In the field of educational administration where decision-making skills are crucial, cases can offer opportunities to practice analysis, problem solving, action planning, and evaluation.

In the educational studies in general and in the area of school administration in particular the interest in the case methodology is manifested through a wide incorporation of and experimentation with case-based instruction in pre-service and in-service training of teachers and administrators. At the university level, special centers have been established for research and promotion of the case methodology in the field of education (Pace University Center for Case Studies in Education is but one example).

Likewise, educational journals devote a great deal of attention to this matter and provide a forum for discussion of the value of case methodology for preparation of educational cadre.

For example, The Journal of Cases in Educational Leadership (JCEL) published by University of Utah is devoted solely to the publication of cases that can be effectively used in preparation of educational leaders. Principal preparation programs have used case studies to remedy problems that arise in the gap between theory and practice.

A major criticism of principal preparation programs has been: "Regardless of the year appointed, have been trained and certified as administrators through programs largely irrelevant to and grossly inadequate for the work responsibilities found in the school principalship". The case methodology combines both artifactual and social elements. The artifactual component is the case itself, a description of an actual situation.

The emergence of computer-based technologies opened up new possibilities for case conferencing. The collision of technology and case methodology was inevitable.

The combination of technology and case-based instruction gave birth to new applications of case methodology in teacher and principal preparation programs, for example video-cases, computer-based simulations, virtual case competitions on the World Wide Web, cases presented as CD-ROM and laser disks, and electronic meeting systems. The technological formats of case analysis can be written, spoken, or based in hypermedia utilizing the Internet or World Wide Web.

Unlike the traditional classroom discussion of cases, electronic meeting systems (EMS) allow for constant ongoing dialogue between participants. Moreover, electronic brainstorming produces significantly more fresh ideas than traditional classroom analysis of cases. EMS also allows more people to interact without interruption and to input ideas simultaneously.

Opportunity for the participation of all group members is also enhanced in computer-mediated case discussions. On-line case discussion in the York University PQP resonates with the need to decrease the gap between classroom instruction and practice and to enhance students' ability to make good decisions that are at the core of school leadership. The PQP on-line cases are experiential narratives that focus on a broad set of concerns specific to the work of the principal.

The cases, referred to by participants as scenarios, problems or situations, are posted weekly by the On-Line Mentors. Each week, candidates read the posted cases and respond to the issues, events and dilemmas of the case taking the perspective of a principal.

This requires them to shift their reading of the cases from their experiential teaching horizon toward a one that encompasses the relationships within the school, the school community and the educational system with it's diverse participants.

The role of case discussion facilitator is important in case methodology generally and the York PQP specifically. The facilitator guides the discussion by probing, directly challenging, or simply observing the discussion process.

Feedback plays an important role in the learning process: as people receive information about the results of their actions, they are able to correct themselves progressively until they achieve the intended results. The PQP On-Line Mentors, all of whom were classroom teachers prior to becoming a principal, bring their knowledge of teaching and learning to the CMC environment.

They provide feedback in the form of comments addressed to candidates' responses, suggestions for different presentation strategies, ideas for deepening the responses, or concluding thoughts. The On-Line Mentors also direct discussions and monitor candidates' participation in order to facilitate discussions that are reflective and thoughtful.

In order to make case discussions challenging, educative and interesting, On-Line Mentors may make suggestions and ask questions related to the posted case. The on-line narratives are written rather than oral interactions, often presented in a laconic and point specific form rather than lengthy and comprehensive manner.

The audiences for whom the narratives are constructed are other educators attending or teaching the course. Although one face-to-face meeting of the on-line groups is scheduled during the course, candidates may never meet their on-line mentor or other members of their on-line group. Group cohesion is developed through a combination of required participation, the skill of the on-line mentor, and the ongoing involvement of the participants.

Case methodology has changed in recent years from the method of instruction based on face-to-face discussion of oral. cases/narratives confined to the classroom space to computer-mediated asynchronous discussion of on-line cases in virtual classrooms/cyber-classrooms.

Narratives in cyberspace, rather than being a part of an oral discourse, entail new communicative styles and ways of engagement with texts/cases on the part of the learners. In theorizing of learning, claims have been made that we learn from the other's response to what we convey.

Thus, learning the art of school leadership through on-line narratives necessitates the learners to put their responses out there and to find out what comes back. A unique feature of the York PQP cases posted on-line is that often they present an account of events that happened in the same week (or sometimes even the same day) as the case is posted for discussion.

While varying in content and length, the cases are authentic narratives from the work experience of GTA principals. As such, they have some pedagogical similarity to more traditional principal training methods such as "inbox" and "shadowing" exercises. Some of the cases posted by On-Line Mentors open up with the words like: "Just a quick situation we had at our school this week that caused us some thought" or "Here is the situation based on a real case that happened recently."

The fact that cases posted for discussion are "fresh" cases enables On-Line Mentors to enrich the dialogue by adding new details and nuances to the case and informing participants about the trajectory of events. The use of narratives brings into view the implicit and explicit ethical and moral issues that permeate the stories of schooling.

Narratives bring the complexity of the coordinated stories about school leadership and administration to the medium of on-line group learning.

Equally important, they allow beginners "to consider and inspect the informal or tacit systems which exist side-by-side with the formal manifest systems operating in schools and organizations'.

One of the program challenges that confront PQP candidates and their program teachers are to develop the skill to see the case narratives through the eyes of an administrator rather than a teacher. In the on-line mentor responses, we see a complex teaching and learning about the social and professional mores of the principalship.

As the course progresses, candidates felt freer to speak from their professional experiences in the teaching profession and from their life experiences as people interested in education.

Bringing their life experiences to bear on an administrative framework, students came up with diverse (often even polar) responses and felt free to disagree with one another.

The consensual uniformity of candidates' standpoints was less present in the analysis of the cases that dealt with ethical concerns or involved moral judgements. The analysis of the PQP on-line narratives, student responses to less complex and more transparent cases often resulted in producing collective virtual texts where each ensuing individual script, more or less, echoed the line of thinking developed in responses posted earlier.

In contrast, the responses to case narratives that drew on local experience with ethical issues embedded in the stories did not turn into unitary, virtual texts—one-best solution—produced by collective efforts of on-line participants. In the United States, Large-scale assessment is undergoing enormous pressure to change. That pressure stems from many causes.

Depending upon the type of test, the issues precipitating change include an outmoded cognitive-scientific basis for test design; a mismatch with curriculum; the differential performance of population groups; a lack of information to help individuals improve; and inefficiency.

These issues provide a strong motivation to reconceptualize both the substance and the business of large-scale assessment. At the same time, advances in technology, measurement, and cognitive science are providing the means to make that reconceptualization a reality.

In the same way that it is already helping to revolutionize commerce, education, and even social interaction, the Internet will help revolutionize the business and substance of large-scale assessment.

Whether for educational admissions, school and student accountability, or public policy, large-scale assessment in the United States is undergoing enormous pressure to change. This pressure is most evident with respect to high-stakes tests, like those used for grade promotion or college entrance. For achievement surveys like NAEP, which offer no information to individuals, schools, or districts, motivation to participate is undoubtedly diminished.

Testing programs are expensive to operate. That expense gets passed on to taxpayers for a state or federal test like NAEP, or directly to examinees in the case of admissions measures.

Further, to be maximally useful, test results are needed quickly. Rapid information delivery is certainly a requirement in the education policy arena, where the results of national surveys may sometimes take years to produce. It is also increasingly true in the admissions context, where more rapid feedback is needed not only for early decisions, financial aid, and the rolling acceptances that are beginning to characterize some distance learning programs, but also for guidance and placement. Radical improvements in assessment will derive from advances in three areas: technology, measurement, and cognitive science.

Of the three, new technology will be the most influential in the short term. New technology will have the greatest influence because it—not measurement and not cognitive science—is pervading our society. Billions of dollars are being invested annually to create and make commonplace powerful, general technologies for commerce, communications, entertainment, and education.

Due to their generality, these technologies can also be used to improve assessment. These technological advancements revolve primarily around the Internet. The Internet is (or will be) interactive, broadband, switched, networked, and standards-based. Interactive means that we can present a task to a student and quickly respond to that student's actions.

Switched means that we can engage in different interactions with different students simultaneously. In combination, these two characteristics (interactive and switched) make for individualized assessments. Broadband means that those interactions can contain lots of information.

For assessment tasks, that information could include audio, video, and animation. Networked indicates that everything is linked. This linkage means that testing agencies, schools, parents, government officials, item writers, test reviewers, human scorers, and students are tied together electronically. That electronic connection can allow for enormous efficiencies. The standards-based means that the network runs according to a set of conventional rules that all participants follow.

That fact permits both the easy interchange of data and access from a wide variety of computing platforms, as long as the software running on those platforms (e.g., Internet browsers), adheres to those rules too. Internet affords the potential to deliver efficiently on a mass scale individualized, highly engaging content to almost any desktop; get data back immediately; process it; and make information available anywhere in the world, anytime day or night. Paper delivery cannot compete with this potential.

The Internet is, of course, not being built to service the needs of large-scale assessment. It is, instead, being built for e-commerce: to sell products and services over the web to consumers and to businesses directly. By any measure, the Internet and use of it, has grown dramatically, to say the least.

As a communications medium, the Internet last year surpassed the telephone, with 3 billion email messages sent each day. The number of unique URLs (web-page directory and subdirectory addresses) has grown from just under a billion in 1998 to a projected 3 billion in 2000. In the United States, the percentage of homes with Internet access has increased from 26% in December 1998 to 42% in August 2000. Worldwide, the number of users has grown from somewhere between 117 to 142 million in 1998 to about 400 million in 2000.

Finally, the number of host computers has gone from about 30 million to 75 million from January 1998 to

January 2000. This phenomenal growth may slow as investment subsides from the speculative rates of the past few years.

However, the vast size of the Internet and its user base constitute a critical mass that should continue to attract substantial capital. For commerce, the promise of the Internet is all about being faster, cheaper, and better. Two "laws" of the digital era illustrate this promise.

Moore's Law predicts the doubling of computational capability (specifically, at the level of the microchip) every 18 months. As Negroponte has explained, what filled a room yesterday is on your desk today and will be on your wrist tomorrow. Metcalfe's Law says that the value of a network increases by the square of the number of people on it. The true value of a network is, thus, less about information and more about community.

One can see this effect clearly in eBay, the online auction broker. Each new user potentially benefits every other existing user because every eBay member can be both buyer and seller. Metcalfe's law is playing out well beyond eBay. Online business-to-business auction brokers are appearing in a variety of industries, including natural gas, electricity, steel, and bandwidth.

Another illustration of this cheaper-faster-better result is the effect of the Internet on the traditional relationship between richness and reach, where richness is the depth of the interaction that a business can have with a customer and reach is the number of customers that a business can contact through a given channel.

Traditionally, one limited the other. That is, a business could attain maximal reach but only limited richness. For example, through direct mail, broadcast, or newspaper ads a company could communicate with many people but have a meaningful interaction with none of them.

Similarly, a business could attain maximal richness but limited reach. Via personal contact (e.g., door-to-door sales), very deep interactions can occur, but with only a relatively small number of people. There are two major dimensions to reinventing assessment.

One is the business of assessment. This dimension centers on the core processes that define an enterprise. In many cases, those core processes can become many times more efficient because moving bits is faster and easier than moving atoms; that is, electronically processing information is far more cost effective than physically manipulating things.

Encyclopaedia Britannica was established in Scotland in 1768. It is the oldest and most famous encyclopedia in the English-speaking world. By 1990, its sales had reached $650 million per annum. But then suddenly, Britannica's fortunes drastically changed.

In 1996, the company was sold for less than half its net worth (i.e., the value of its assets, including its encyclopedia inventory, minus its liabilities). That same year, it eliminated its entire door-to-door North American sales force.

What happened was that the reference book business was reinvented because of the emergence of new technology. At its peak, Britannica was a 32-volume set of books costing well over $1,000. In 1993, Microsoft introduced Encarta on CD-ROM for under $100 and even though Britannica was much more comprehensive, the difference for most people wasn't worth an extra $900+.

Initially, Britannica did not respond as it didn't take the threat from Encarta seriously. But when it did respond, it did so ineffectively because Britannica wouldn't fit on a single CD-ROM and because the company's large sales force wasn't suited to selling software. But, ultimately, Britannica wasn't ready to cannibalize its existing paper business to enter this new electronic one.

It's important because similar (though less extreme) scenarios are playing themselves out now in individual investing, book selling, travel planning, music distribution, long distance telephony, and even business-to-business transactions. These reinvention scenarios are forcing organizations—including some in educational assessment—to come quickly to grips with where new technology will and will not help core business processes.

As should be obvious, technology-driven changes in business processes can occur quickly and their consequences can be significant for the organizations that service a particular market.

In fact, if radical and pervasive enough, process changes can force shifts in the substance of the business itself. So, although reinventing the business of assessment by incorporating technology into specific assessment processes is about trying to achieve the efficiencies needed to remain competitive today, reinventing the substance of assessment—most fundamentally, the reason we do it—is not about today.

The populations seeking education are changing and so are their purposes for learning. At the college level, just 16% of students fit the traditional profile: 18-22 years old, full-time, on-campus resident. This is not because fewer 18-22 year olds are going to college. It is because more adults are. The adult cohort is, in fact, the fastest growing segment in postsecondary education. Working adults over age 24 constitute some 44% of college students. Over the past 25 years, employer demand in the U.S. has shifted toward higher educational qualifications, as indicated by an increasing premium paid for those with a college degree.

But in addition to this rise in entry qualifications, the knowledge required to maintain a job in many occupations is changing so fast that 50% of all employees' skills are estimated to become outdated within 3-5 years. Witness any job that requires interaction with information technology (IT), which is a growing proportion of jobs.

In fact, by 2006 almost half of all workers will be employed by industries that are either major producers or intensive users of IT products and services. So, more people want postsecondary education because they need to have it if they want to become—and stay—employed.

And, more of these individuals are nontraditional students who may work, travel in their jobs, or have families. This population's unmet educational need is increasingly becoming the target of distance learning. According to the National Center for Education Statistics, between fall 1995 and 1997-98, the percentage of higher education institutions offering distance learning courses increased by one-third, and the number of course offerings and enrollments approximately doubled.

But although many institutions have delivered distance learning via mail, radio, or television for years, this growth is not in those media. Rather, it is distance learning via the Internet that is booming. Among all higher-education institutions offering any distance learning, the percentage of institutions using asynchronous Internet-based technologies nearly tripled, from 22% in 1995 to 60% in 1997-1998.

More recent data from Market Data Retrieval (MDR) confirm the trend. MDR relates that, as of the 1999-2000 academic year, 34% of two- and four-year colleges offered accredited degree programs via computer, up from 15% the year before.

As of 2000, U.S. institutions reportedly offered more than 6,000 accredited courses on the Web and, by 2002, over 2 million students will be enrolled, a tripling of the 1998 enrollment. At the same time, Internet-based distance learning is finding its way into high school. The need is generated by home-schooled students (of which there are over 1 million in the US), districts without a full complement of qualified teachers, and the children of migrant workers.

So-called "virtual high schools" have emerged in Alabama, Arizona, California, Florida, Illinois, Indiana, Kentucky, Maryland, Massachusetts, Michigan, Missouri, Nebraska, New Mexico, and Utah. These programs can cross state lines, with offerings open to students regardless of residence. Of particular note is that both the University of Missouri at Columbia High School and the Indiana University High School have been granted accreditation by the North Central Association of Colleges and Schools.

Accreditation means that students can apply course grades earned through these online institutions toward their high-school graduation. The growth of Internet-based distance learning will have a significant impact upon traditional education. For one, it may threaten the existence of established institutions.

Many in the private sector see education as a huge industry that produces mediocre results for a high cost. If the private sector can leverage new technologies, like distance learning, to deliver greater value, the institutions that dominate education today will not be the leaders tomorrow. The rapid growth of for-profit education companies, and the seemingly endless creation of well-capitalized new ones, suggests that a serious challenge to the existing order is well underway.

The gravity of the threat is evident in how non-profits have responded. A second reason that the growth of Internet-based distance learning will influence traditional education is that regardless of its impact on nonprofit institutions, the distance learning industry will produce sophisticated software that everyone can use, in school and out. The considerable potential of online learning—local or distance—is reflected in a report to the President and Congress of the bipartisan Web-Based Education Commission.

The question is no longer if the Internet can be used to transform learning in new and powerful ways. The Commission has found that it can. Nor is the question should we invest the time, the energy, and the money necessary to fulfill its promise in defining and shaping new learning opportunity.

As online learning becomes more widespread, the substance and format of assessment will need to keep pace. So, as students do more and more of their learning using technology tools, asking them to express that learning in a medium different from the one they typically work in will become increasingly untenable, especially where working with the medium is part of the skill being tested. These changes in learning methodology offer exciting possibilities for assessment innovation.

On site or off, an obvious result of delivering courses via the Internet is the potential for embedding assessment, perhaps almost seamlessly, in instruction. Since students respond to instructional exercises electronically, their responses can be recorded, leaving a continuous learning trace.

Depending upon how the course and the assessment are designed, this information could conceivably support a sophisticated model of student proficiencies. That model might be useful both for dynamically deciding what instruction to present next and for making more global judgments about what the student knows and can do at any given point.

In addition to assessment embedded in Internet-delivered courses, one can imagine Internet-delivered-assessment embedded in traditional classroom activity. Such assessment might take the form of periodically delivered exercises that both teach and test. In this scenario, the exercises would be standardized and performance might serve, depending upon the level of aggregation, to indicate individual, classroom, school, district, state, or national achievement.

Thus, these exercises could serve summative as well as formative purposes and be useful to individuals as well as institutions. A continuing concern with such reinvention visions is whether schools (and students) are ready technologically and, in particular, what to do about technology differences across social groups.

The National Center for Education Statistics (NCES) reports that as of September 1999, 95% of schools were connected to the Internet, up from 35% in 1994. Schools in all categories, (i.e., by grade level, poverty concentration, and metropolitan status), were equally likely to have Internet access. Further, most schools had dedicated lines: only 14% were using dial-up modem, a slower and less reliable access method.

Clearly many of these schools could have only a single connected machine and that machine could be the one sitting on the principal's desk. According to NCES, as of September 1999, 63% of all instructional rooms had Internet access (up from 3% in 1994, a 20-fold increase in five years).

The ratio of students to Internet-connected computers was 9:1, down from 12:1 only a year earlier. These are staggering numbers, for they imply that classrooms are connecting to the Internet at a very rapid rate. This success is in no small part due to federal efforts.

The government's e-rate program has been giving public schools and libraries discounts of up to 90% on phone service, Internet hook-ups, and wiring for several years. In total, the program has committed 3.65 billion dollars to over 50,000 institutions, helping connect more than one million public school classrooms.

In addition, 70% of the program's last round of funding went to schools in the lowest income areas. However, even with these very significant efforts, there continue to be equity issues. As of September 1999, in high poverty schools, the ratio of students to Internet computers was 16 to 1. Certainly, with few exceptions, it would be impossible to deliver large-scale assessment via the Internet today. But the trend is clear: the infrastructure is quickly falling into place for Internet delivery of assessment to schools, perhaps first in survey programs like NAEP that require only a small participant sample from each school, but eventually for inclusive assessments delivered directly to the desktop. As evidence, witness the requests-for-proposals recently released by the state education departments of Oregon, Virginia, and Georgia for building Internet-delivered, state-assessment systems.

Clearly, more students are becoming computer-familiar every day and developing such skills is a national educational technology goal. But, as Negroponte suggests, computer familiarity is really the wrong issue. The secret to good interface design is to make it go away. Thus, advances in technology will eventually eliminate the need to be computer familiar. After nomadic computing, which we are now entering with the proliferation of wireless Internet devices and personal digital assistants, comes ubiquitous computing—the embedding of new technology into everyday items.

Inventions like "radio" paper may allow students to interact with computers in the same way that they interact with paper today. Smart desks are another likelihood, in which case a test may be electronically delivered, quite literally, to every desktop.

In the U. S., then, we may see a future in which every classroom is wired and every student can easily take tests on line. To be sure, the Internet is an American phenomenon. It derives from research sponsored by the Defense Department in the 1960's.

These nations have the telecommunications infrastructure and citizens with enough disposable income to afford the trappings of Internet use. The challenges for these nations are undoubtedly great. Over time, however, we should see significant progress in building the infrastructure and the user base here too.

This progress will occur for at least two reasons. First, the cost of technology has been dropping precipitously and, by Moore's law, will continue to decline. Further, because the future of computing is undoubtedly in wireless devices, a telecommunications infrastructure will be much cheaper to acquire than the land-lines of old. Metcalfe's law suggests, markets will become all the more valuable as they are interconnected.

That developing nations join the e-commerce network means greater opportunity for all. It means more vendor choice for the people of developing nations; more opportunity for developed nations to serve these markets; and a new opportunity for third-world businesses themselves to compete globally. The Internet will make it easier for developing nations to get access to assessment services from elsewhere and for those nations to distribute their own assessment services regionally or around the world.

This ease of access and distribution should make it possible to form international consortia. Such consortia will be able to assemble technical resources that a single nation might not be able to acquire. In addition, those consortia may be able to purchase services from others more efficiently than nations could obtain individually.

Finally, an electronic network should make it easier to participate in international studies, bringing the benefits of benchmarking to nations throughout the world. One of the largest instantiations of technology-based assessment to date is computer-based testing (CBT) in postsecondary admissions.

As programs like the Graduate Record Examinations, the Graduate Management Admission Test, and the Test of English as a Foreign Language have found, CBT can be enormously costly. Being among the first large-scale programs to move to computer, they bore the brunt of creating the infrastructure for what was essentially a new business.

The building of that infrastructure was initiated in the early 1990's before test developers knew how to create tests for computer, before computers were widely available for individuals to take tests on, and before the Internet was ready to bring those tests to students. In essence, these programs needed to build both a factory to stamp out a new product and a new distribution mechanism.

A first generation infrastructure now exists, but it is not yet optimized to produce and deliver tests as efficiently as possible. If we have learned anything from the history of innovation, it is that new technologies are often initially far too expensive for mass use.

That was true of the automobile, telephone service, commercial aviation, and the personal computer, among many other innovations. For example, in 1930 the cost of a three-minute telephone call from New York to London was $250. By 1995, the cost had dropped to under $1. As a second instance, when the IBM Personal Computer was introduced in 1981, it cost around $5,000.

At the time, the median family income in the United States was on the order of $25,000, so that a computer cost about 20% of the average family's earnings—not very affordable. At this writing, the cost of a computer with many times greater capability is a little more than $500 and the median income is closer to $55,000. A computer now costs about 1% of average income.

When a promising new technology appears, individuals and institutions invest, allowing the technology to evolve and a supporting infrastructure to develop. Over the course of that development, failures inevitably occur.

Eventually, the technology either dies or becomes commercially viable—that is, efficient enough. At this point, it's an impressive list including non-profit testing agencies, for profit-testing companies, school districts, state education departments, government agencies, and companies with no history in testing at all.

Sustaining technologies enhance the performance of established products in ways that mainstream customers have traditionally valued. Historically, most technological advances in any given industry have been sustaining ones (e.g., in the personal computer industry, faster chips and bigger, higher-resolution monitors). Occasionally, disruptive technologies emerge. Companies introduce these technologies hoping their features will provide competitive edge.

However, these features characteristically overshoot the market, giving customers more than they need or are willing to pay for. Thus, disruptive technologies result in worse product performance, at least in the near-term, on key dimensions in a company's established markets. Interestingly, a few fringe customers typically find a disruptive technology's new features attractive.

In these niche markets, such technology may thrive. If and when it advances to the level and nature of performance demanded in the mainstream market, the new technology can invade it, rapidly knocking out the traditional technology and its dependent practitioners. CBT has many of the characteristics of a disruptive technology. Established testing organizations are applying it in their mainstream markets, most notably postsecondary admissions.

This innovation was introduced, in good part, to provide competitive edge through features like the ability to take a test at one's convenience and to get score reports immediately. As it turned out, these features overshot the market. At least initially, registrations for continuously-offered computer-based admissions tests mirrored those for fixed-date administrations, suggesting that scheduling convenience was not a highly valued feature in the market of the time.

Moreover, examinees were dissatisfied with losing some of the features of paper exams, including the ability to proceed through the test nonlinearly, the option to review the scoring of items actually taken, and the low cost.

Although it encountered difficulty in the mainstream admissions testing market, CBT found more rapid acceptance in the niches. One example is information technology (IT) certification, which individuals pursue to document their competence in some computer-related proficiency.

In 1999, over three million examinations in 25 languages were administered in this market. Most of these tests were delivered on computer and most were offered on a continuous basis. Let's start by asking what features a testing product must have to succeed in this niche. First, it must be continuously offered because these test candidates build technology skill on their own schedules—at home or on the job, very often through books or online learning. These individuals want to test when they are ready, not when the testing companies are. Second, such a test must generally be offered on computer since technology use is the essence of the certification.

Lower security is tolerable because if an individual appears on the job with a dishonestly obtained credential but without the required skill, he or she will not last. Finally, test volume is self-replicating: there are many repeat test takers because information technology changes rapidly, so skills must be updated constantly. From an innovation perspective, then, IT certification may be one context in which the CBT of today can flourish and develop to better meet the needs of other assessment markets.

Industry leaders often fail precisely because they attempt to introduce disruptive technologies into major markets before it's time. The Industry leaders do not pursue those opportunities to refine the technology. Instead, they give up, having run out of resources or credibility. Making a disruptive technology work requires iteration and iteration means failure.

The online learning will become a major enterprise, especially for the lifelong updating of skills. In this market, institutions will be less concerned with questions of who gets in and more with who gets out, and what it is they have to do to get out.

Similarly, individuals are becoming more concerned with finding course offerings that meet their skill development goals and less with whether those offerings come from one institution or a half-dozen. The assessment need at first, it is for knowledge facilitation and, second, for knowledge certification; that is, to help people develop their skills and then document that they've developed them. The challenge is to figure out how to design and deliver embedded assessment that provides instructional support and that globally summarizes learning accomplishment.

Ethical Issues

Ethical issues are surprisingly often lurking in technical decisions. For example, reporting outcomes from a continuous measure in terms of the percent of students who surpassed a certain level, produces unethical behavior: a concentration of teaching on borderline students.

Distortion of behavior and data corruption are ever-present concerns in indicator systems. The systems we describe would have probably failed to thrive had they not addressed schools' on-going concerns about education. Moreover, data interpretation can only be completed in the schools, by those who know all the factors involved. Over the last 15 years, indicator systems that have developed, and attracted support and subscriptions from about a third of the schools in England where we work on a scale many times greater than any other group.

And also developed a linked Curriculum, Evaluation and Management Centre at the University of Canterbury in Christchurch, New Zealand, and have the pleasure of welcoming participation from scattered schools in thirty countries. The development of the indicator systems in the CEM Centre is unusual if not unique in that schools themselves have chosen to participate. The systems are therefore professional, ground-up, developments, that stand in contrast to "top-down" indicator systems created, and sometimes imposed, by state and local authorities.

The interests of both kinds of systems should ultimately, however, be coincident: to improve education. An indicator can be defined as an item of information collected at regular intervals to track the performance of a system. The indicator systems that have formed the basis of our learning are all designed to feed back valuable information of interest to teachers and administrators in schools and colleges.

The indicator or information systems as significantly empowering schools as they participate with a university in 'distributed research'. The issue of public accountability must also addressed by indicator systems. The design of each system has been driven by the need to measure outcomes that matter along with relevant covariates so that fair comparisons can be made.

Process variables are measured in some of the systems, but only to generate hypotheses, not to make judgements. In 1997, Fitz-Gibbon can be found on the website for the Qualifications and Curriculum Authority. Technical issues include those procedural problems that must be solved if an indicator system is to be of high quality and run in a timely, efficient and effective fashion.

Indicators need to be based on adequate samples, have appropriate levels of reliability, good validity, and above all, positive reactivity. These are technical terms straight out of research methods courses, but they go to the heart of indicator systems, and any practical use of data. The data must be of research quality, otherwise it will confuse rather than guide. In 1983, technical sophistication was no more than batch-processing using a mainframe.

The mainframe could deliver capital letters and stars and eventually an adequate type-face could be constructed via embedded commands in a special program that could produce quite nicely spaced upper and lower case printing.

Access to a data entry service was essential and it was quickly obvious, as the volume of data increased, that adequate data verification techniques had to be built-in. At first, this was by double-entry, which was not satisfactory; followed by data checking on entry, which required some programming to prevent out-of-range data being entered and to ensure the data went into the right columns on the 80-column cards.

From these humble and clumsy beginnings, today to a situation where extensive programming is used, optical mark recognition assists some data entry, computer based tests that can record responses directly and be delivered across intranets and internets are becoming essential features of indicator systems. Not only is data translated into meaningful sentences contingent upon the data-values, but also into graphs that, for example, change colour when differences are statistically significant.

Without this level of technical expertise, data will not be attractive and easy to access by busy teachers, the turn-around of data will be slow and errors will creep in. Schools want data quickly, within weeks of examination results becoming available. And they want the data 100 per cent accurate. In most research projects, if a small percentage of the data doesn't match, this can simply be reported and ignored, but in indicator systems, schools want every single student accounted for.

In consequence, not only must there be teams of expert programmers, but also very high capacity computing equipment. Facilities for printing CDs are helpful, as special, user-friendly software is developed to assist schools in their own explorations of their data. CDs can also be used to deliver computerised tests. data files returned to schools also need to interface easily with schools' management information software such as timetabling and staff deployment.

If the technical infrastructure is effective, data turn-around quick, data presentation attractive and readily interpreted, then the indicator systems will probably grow and this growth itself demands further technical capabilities, such as running a high-capacity server and creating a central database that can be accessed by researchers and secretaries alike. This central database needs to be relational in order to store efficiently the hundreds of thousands of students with hundreds of variables attached to each student in thousands of schools over many years.

It must have an extremely friendly front end, so that secretaries can readily track the mail-out of questionnaires and the return of data, plus a massive invoicing system if individual schools can join the project and pay on their own account.

Finally the infrastructure needs communication on a regular basis with all schools. Newsletters, a website and conferences are important, particularly as teachers become conference presenters and have a credibility with fellow teachers that researchers lose after some years away from the classroom. If the infrastructure for indicator systems can be created, then a cost-effective system is feasible.

It consider the design of such a system, including choosing what to measure, collecting the data, analysing, reporting and interpreting the data. A few indicators cannot reflect the complexity of institutions and will undermine the system as gaming takes hold. Given a few indicators, the effort is focused on these concerns alone. Furthermore it is difficult to know which indicators will become important in the future, so that what is now considered to be a key indicator may become of less concern in the future.

Multiple indicators for complex organisations are a fairer representation of the multiple realities within each than is any attempt to assign a single label, whether this label be numerical (e.g. average value added) or verbal (e.g. 'coasting', 'failing'). The essence of schooling is who is taught what for how long and by what methods and these concerns can, following the OECD practice be called 'Flow'. Eventually all of these aspects should have indicators.

The indicators could be collected from various groups such as students, teachers, heads, school districts, states, or parents, the community, the voters. Most indicators could be an input, an output or a long-term outcome and may also be related to a process.

Thus a comprehensive classification of indicators can be developed and this also will require a relational database if the measures are to be efficiently stored. Prior achievement is an excellent predictor of subsequent achievement, but each student's level of prior achievement will be partly influenced by the effectiveness of the previous stage of schooling. One teacher's output is then another teacher's input.

Teachers quite reasonably worry that if they promote high achievement at one age it may be more difficult to show high rates of progress (value added) subsequently. The introduction of baseline tests as an alternative to achievement input measures has provided an important alternative approach.

The purpose of our baseline tests is not to stamp labels on students, but to predict how easy or difficult it will be to get students through the next set of examinations. What is needed for these tests, then, is typical performance, not maximum performance. In the secondary school use tape recordings for test administration so that all schools present students with the same information in the same tone of voice using exactly the same words and the same timing of each of the subtests.

The baseline tests to obtain good predictions of subsequent achievement. The aim has been to obtain quick and efficient measures by using item formats and tasks that require many responses from the pupil that are instantly recorded and therefore add up very quickly to a good predictor of general academic performance. These tests are in some cases remarkably efficient.

The best source of information about relevant covariates is not what people write about, but what the data shows. Much is written, for example, of the impact of socio-economic status on achievement, but at the pupil level the correlation is generally about 0.3, thus implying that about 9 per cent of variance in the outcomes will be accounted for by knowing the socio-economic status of the student. In contrast, cognitive measures predict about 50 per cent of subsequent variation.

To obtain adequate prediction of subsequent achievement ... and therefore the fairest data for teachers...there is no adequate alternative to a cognitive test. In addition to the cognitive indicators we need to address the affective and social domains.

In Victoria, Australia, there is extensive use of questionnaires to students, to staff in schools and to parents. Currently, in the Curriculum, Evaluation and Management Centre, concentrate on questionnaires to students, since education is primarily aimed at the students who are compulsory under the treatment indicator systems.

Students can tell questionnaires how much they like school, how much they like an individual subject, whether they feel safe in school, their aspirations for the future, their relationships with teachers, their health, traumas in their lives, how they are taught, and how interesting they find each subject, etc., etc. For children in their first year at school also ask teachers to rate the children's attention, impulsivity and activity levels.

Certainly, when schools first join an indicator system, they can feel quite overwhelmed by the amount of data that is returned from a fully developed system. For schools in the first few years of participation 'Keep it simple, stupid' might be a good motto, especially as there is evidence that giving people too much data is de-motivating. Another wide variety of systems of indicators that involve paper- or computer-based tests, as well as 'basic' or 'extended' versions, the latter including hundreds of variables.

The system that will involve on-line administration of data collection and permit matrix sampling and the inclusion of choice, by students or other respondents to questionnaires, of the domains in which they would like to express their views and opinions. This will need close attention to the reliability of the data collected. Thus the matrix sampling will use scales as the unit of sampling rather than items. Having decided on how to measure the outcomes that matter, one is not finished with the creation of indicators.

Just as prior achievement predicts subsequent achievement, so prior attitudes will predict subsequent attitudes, and in order to compare like with like need to use regression analyses and look at the residuals. The prediction appears not to be so strong as in the cognitive area, perhaps due to less reliable measures, but about 25 percent of the variance of final attitudes in secondary schools is usually predictable from knowing intake attitudes.

An indicator system consisting of dependent variables with appropriate covariates is a complete indicator system. However, an indicator system is only a step along the way to trying to understand what works, and how schooling can be improved.

Consequently, some of the indicator systems include process variables such as descriptions of methods of teaching and learning for which students in the 16-18 age range report the frequency of use.

Process indicators serve to generate hypotheses and most importantly, they stimulate discussion of teaching methods among staff in schools and as such are valuable. The cognitive data collection is standardised so that the same procedures are followed in every school. This standardisation of data collection is important in collecting data that can be validly compared from school to school.

A particular threat to the validity of attitude data could arise from demand characteristics. If students are being asked if they like the school and whether they get on well with teachers yet teachers are looking over students' shoulders, or if the students feel that their questionnaires will be scrutinised by teachers, then the situation becomes subject to possible pressures and influences that could inhibit honest responding. The creation of a monitoring system involves a great many decisions and, as a system grows and there is feedback from the users of the system, there is a need to be responsive and flexible whilst holding firm to fundamental principles. In developing an on-entry assessment for 4-5 year olds the intention was that the data would be kept until the children reached the first statutory assessment three years later.

But many reception class teachers suggested that we should assess the students again at the end of their first year at school using an extended version of the on-entry assessment. The outcome measures should, of course, be curriculum-embedded, high-stakes, authentic tests that reflect work actually taught and worth teaching in the classroom.

The use of a standardised multiple choice measure of reading comprehension, for example, is not likely to be fair to schools since teachers may not be able to influence reading comprehension skills once students can read. In other words, there is a problem of lack of sensitivity to instruction.

The matching of data from different sources can only be efficiently done by the use of unique identifiers. These preferably should be identifiers containing check digits and the computing facilities to make sure that no identifier is mis-entered. Einstein said that everything should be as simple as possible, but no simpler.

The multi-level analysis, requiring special software and a postgraduate course in statistical analysis, was in contrast to the ordinary least squares analysis that could be taught in primary schools. In UK, the ordinary least squares analysis can certainly be presented to schools so that most members of staff understand the analysis and can use software to re-analyse data as necessary.

This accessibility of the data along with the atmosphere of joint investigation probably helped to encourage acceptance of the indicator systems, unlike the situation that sadly seems to have arisen in Tennessee where a highly ambitious, yearly multi-level analysis was tracking students and teachers. The development of multilevel modelling or hierarchical linear models is admirable, provides efficient calculations and rather different error terms, but to use these procedures in day to day indicator system work is likely to lead to less acceptance of the analysis by teachers. Moreover, it is somewhat akin to applying a correction for relativity when considering the momentum of a moving train: theoretically correct, but in scientific terms, an ill-advised tendency to over-precision.

The essence of good statistical modelling is to model the process that produces the data. From the very start, with the A Level Information System in 1982-83, it was clear that the regression line for mathematics was quite different from the regression line for English and implied that for the same level of prior achievement students would come out with two grades lower taking the Advanced examination in mathematics than they would taking Advanced English.

Regrettably, other researchers have simply taken the results of all examinations and assumed that the scales could be combined without any adjustment. Having thus confused the data, sophisticated multilevel models were applied to find that there were differential slopes, i.e. slopes that differed for high and low ability intakes.

It was even suggested that teachers may be to blame for concentrating on some groups more than others. This was poor data interpretation since a confound (different subjects with different regression lines) was being attributed to teachers' actions without any corroborating evidence. The presentation of data needs to change according to the experience of the school.

A school just beginning to get feedback data needs a few clear diagrams and a telephone helpline in case of questions. Schools that have become used to receiving data and have, despite some initial rejection from some departments found it to be useful and credible, start to make more and more use of the data. It therefore becomes valuable to them to have the data provided in Excel spreadsheets, possibly with pre-programmed macros, or in specially prepared software that allows them to undertake procedures such as separating out teaching groups, aggregating by curriculum area, dropping students who have missed substantial amounts of schooling, and adding students for whom data was missing.

Eventually, with tight encryption techniques this will be directly over the internet. It has been important, for example, that baseline tests are not seen as predicting exact outcomes.

Fifty per cent of the variation in outcomes is predictable but that means that 50 per cent is not. This problem was confronted very early in that schools were in some cases preventing students from taking advanced mathematics had they not received a C grade or higher in earlier mathematics courses.

When data from a large number of schools was available, in some of which students had been allowed to take the advanced course even having not done well earlier, it was possible to present what we now call 'Chances graphs'. This empirical distribution has great credibility with teachers and students. It is data that actually happened and if it happened once it can happen again. Thus, the low-achieving student is encouraged to recognise that many low achieving students from the previous year well exceeded the average predicted grade for that starting point.

By representing their 'chances', we remove the opposition rightly felt to labelling students with single predicted grades and provide actual data that is motivating for students. Compliance with freedom of information legislation and other relevant laws may require that considerable amounts of data are published. The issue as to what should be published is taken up later since it raises ethical issues.

Taken under genuine examination conditions, with revision time having been invested and the adrenaline flowing, students might well be producing much better results than those calibrated. Hence the unconscious drift in 'standards'. It is an unusual teacher-training course that prepares teachers for the kind of information that is now available in England through professional monitoring systems.

And yet the information is now seen as vital to many educational professionals. The enormous need for in-service work is an essential part of any monitoring system and that the extent of the need for conferences and workshops often only becomes apparent as the project starts running. A school may implement an innovation and the indicator suggests worse results. But perhaps the results would have been even worse without the innovation. Epidemiology and clinical trials both have their virtues, but the clinical trials are necessary to establish sound evidence as to what works.

That concept applies in education as in medicine and the term 'evidence-based' is now becoming popular. As 'value-added' became the popular word for residuals, evidence-based may become the popular word for experiments.

A major ethical imperative is to do good rather than to do harm. At the very least we might try to observe the Hippocratic oath and 'at least do no harm'. Evidence of the likely impact of indicator systems on participating schools will be considered including the small number of controlled trials that exist. The effect of the randomly assigned feedback was measured not against no feedback but against already substantial feedback, so to expect any further improvement was perhaps optimistic.

Nevertheless as a result of giving classroom by classroom analyses to the teachers concerned, rather than simply departmental data from which this information could be extracted. In the Years Late Secondary Information System, a list of under-aspiring students is produced by combining students' intentions regarding continuing in education with their baseline scores. Many schools given the list of under-aspiring students set up mentoring sessions or special monitoring.

Unfortunately, good intentions do not guarantee good outcomes. Aware of the ethical responsibility not to have teachers wasting their time and in order to avoid harming students, we obtained permission from some schools to only feed back to them a random half of the list of their under-aspiring students. In England, where external curriculum-embedded assessments have been used for decades and school performance tables are published using raw results, moves have been made towards value added systems.

These will increase the high stakes nature of the external examinations and, at the same time, government pressure on the Qualifications and Curriculum Authority has led to a reduction from seven independent examination boards to three conglomerates of the former boards. Furthermore there has been a reduction in the number of syllabuses on offer for secondary schools.

in primary schools, a single National Curriculum has been imposed and all primary students sit the same tests designed to the same syllabuses at the ages of 7, 11 and 14 years. The specification of a National Curriculum concentrating on particular subjects and the publication of these data has put schools under pressure to drop attention to such areas as the fine arts, the performing arts, and physical education, and to concentrate on those indicators that are published.

All schools are forced to do the same curriculum unless exemptions are granted. This restriction and concentration certainly represents a downgrading of the professional status of teachers who can now make few important decisions, and it may contribute to declining levels of satisfaction of teachers. At the very least there should be various curricula available to be chosen, as was the case for decades for teachers of students aged 16 and 18 years.

Thus, a teacher who preferred to teach physical geography rather than economic geography could find a syllabus in which the proportion was attractive for that teacher. Another reason for maintaining choice and diversity in syllabuses is that in the entire population a much broader range of skills is thereby likely to be developed. Choice and diversity also keep the examination boards in competition and this ought to lead to an improvement in the quality of the service that they provide.

Unfortunately, since they have a virtual monopoly endowed by government approval, it will not be likely that examination boards drop their poor practice unless required to do so. Examples of poor practice from examination boards are leaving the names of students and their schools on the examination paper when it is being assessed.

The name of the pupil and the school will often contain clear evidence regarding the pupil's gender, ethnicity, social class and religion. There may be differences between groups, but ethnicity is very poorly defined; socio-economic status is not well-measured; and neither of these variables, is alterable by the school. Religion is perhaps an alterable variable, but Catholic schools are doing better than Protestant schools. The habit of analysing by these unalterable variables may simply be a result of the pressure to produce academic papers, whether they contribute to practical or theoretical developments or not.

The fact that such analyses perpetuate stereotyping should also be a matter of ethical concern. That these correlational analyses do not promote the search for strong evidence as to what works, is certainly a matter for ethical concern.

Attention should be directed towards alterable variables rather than unalterable categories into which human beings are grouped, which is the first step to stereotyping.

These analyses become particularly a matter of concern when teachers are presumed to be somehow to blame for the 'under-achievement' of boys at the age of 16 as compared with the achievement of girls. Group differences make catchy headlines in the newspapers.

While there may sometimes be a need to track group differences, there is a more important need to educate users of data about the size of the effects being studied and what is known about altering the situation. In England, official bodies such as the Office for Standards in Education, lacking pupil level value added measures, compare schools with 'similar' schools.

The classification of 'similar' is usually made on the basis of the percent of students receiving free school meals. However, two schools can both have 20 per cent of students receiving free school meals but otherwise have quite different profiles. For example, one may have a larger proportion of children who also come from schools with very high levels of achievement. Such a school benchmarked against a school with the same percent of free school meals will look very good at the expense of the other school, but the comparison is spurious.

Such benchmarking is an inadequate way of making comparisons. The only fair comparisons are with similar students in other schools. It is certainly not ethical to make unfair comparisons which in some cases carry financial consequences for the institution concerned and can lead to job losses and demoralisation.

Indeed, to take a most extreme and serious consequence, Ofsted inspectors rely on poor benchmarking data and also sit in classrooms judging teachers. In short, whole school indicators should be avoided because the evidence is that there is more variation within a single school than is generally found between schools.

Furthermore, the use of whole school indicators encourages the rank ordering of schools and the public is not prepared to interpret rank orders adequately. Very small differences in the indicator can move a school through many positions in a rank ordering in the middle of a distribution.

Indicator systems, feasible because of computers, may make the public sector, and in particular public sector management, a fascinating exercise in applied social science.

Finally social scientists may have some responsibility for more than arguments and papers. The actions of managers and administrators should be guided by social science findings.

In the digital age, educational materials, whether supplemental course materials or whole online courses, are able to transcend geographical barriers. The frontiers of higher education institutions are no longer defined by commuting distances or national boundaries. Instead, their reach is now more fluid, and is increasingly shaped by the local availability of communications technologies, language skills, commonalities of interest and un-met demand in far off places.

Informational and communication technologies are transforming the ways in which teachers teach and students learn. An insight into the issues that arise at the intersection of these changes, when new frontiers, new technologies and new pedagogies meet.

Focusing on developments in Singapore, Malaysia and Vietnam, it explores some of the sociocultural implications of the internationalisation that results from the use of new technologies in higher education. The use of educational technology is significantly altering access to higher education.

New technologies are lessening geographical barriers to education. Individuals and institutions with access to the Internet have an enormous volume of educational materials at their disposal, regardless of their physical location.

However, such access comes at a price, and the need for expensive hardware, software and telecommunications poses a serious financial barrier for much of the population of the region. Academics in poor countries such as Vietnam are beginning to obtain Internet access, which allows them to keep up to date with international developments in the field, access publications and maintain international networks of colleagues. This requirement is increasing infrastructure costs for educational institutions, which is particularly difficult for public institutions in poor countries. This also creates new barriers to entry for prospective students, who are increasingly required to have independent access to computer equipment and Internet access.

The geographical centre-periphery divide in education is slowly being replaced by a digital divide between those who can afford to participate in global information networks and those who cannot. The use of information and communication technologies in education is expanding access to information, educational products and whole courses, which are coming to form a globalised information network.

Access to these technologies is a precondition for participation in a global information society. Clearly, individuals and institutions that are able to access and participated in these global networks are at an advantage.

However, there are, of course, huge disparities in access to information and communications technologies. In recent years, inequalities in access to new information and communications technologies have become increasingly apparent. On a global scale, the cosmopolitanism of the wealthy is in stark contrast to the localism of the poor.

With economic globalisation, increasingly the wealthy have ready access to global communications media, work for companies with branches in many countries, have colleagues and clients from different cultural backgrounds, travel regularly for business and pleasure, and generally think, feel and act transnationally. The groups which are 'information rich' in the sense that they have ready access to information and communications technology, also possess a worldview that is disembedded enough from the particularities of local conditions to allow them to traverse the cultural differences of a global arena with relative ease.

In wealthier societies, such as Australia, the United States and Singapore, a large proportion of the population have access to such networks. Public education systems in these countries are connected to global flows of information, albeit with inferior machines and lower bandwidth than the private education sector.

In poorer countries, much smaller segments of the popular are able to participate. Public education systems are stretched providing more basic services across the country, while private education institutions offer those who can afford it an entry point into the global information society. The United States have detailed the extent of inequalities in access to computers and the Internet in that country. Even within wealthy societies such as the United States, there is a clear relationship between socioeconomic status, computer ownership and Internet access. This is not to imply that one can draw a neat line between those with computers and online and those without computers and offline.

Nevertheless, whether socioeconomic status is measured according to income, race or educational attainment, the same patterns appear-socially advantaged groups are also technologically advantaged. This is to be expected, but the implications of this distribution for the equity and access to online education, and for the character of the emerging markets in educational services have been largely ignored by educational institutions.

The American College Board concludes that 'the result of the new technologies may be to deepen the divide between educational haves and have-nots, and that the marketplace alone will not fix the problem. Public policy must intervene to narrow the 'digital divide' between whites and minorities, the wealthy and the less advantaged.'

These inequalities are not likely to be addressed by the market because educational providers are currently competing to attract those students who can afford the technology and enrolment fees to their new courses.

On an international level, the inequalities are starker, as are the implications. Within a nation, governments can be persuaded that they have a responsibility to ensure fairer access to new media in education. For example, in the United States the Clinton government has taken steps to provide financial aid to ensure public access to groups who cannot afford to privately acquire the technology.

In addition to egalitarian concerns, there is a strong national economic imperative driving this effort to provide broad access to learning technology. Similar policies have been adopted by most wealthy nations, as much out of eagerness to universalise the reach of emerging technologies, expand their high-tech industries and train a large high-tech labour force as out of a concern with educational equality.

In the international arena, however, there are no equivalent transnational entities that have the ability to redress inequalities in access to technology to provide wider access to the fruits of the Information Age. Much of the world's population do not have access to the most basic communication technologies, such as postal services and telephones, either because these are not available, not reliable or are prohibitively expensive. In less technologically developed regions, differentials in access to information and communication technologies are stark. While a small number of educational institutions are benefiting from the introduction of new technologies, the majority who do not have access find themselves further behind than they were before.

For example, in Malaysia, while the Smart Schools program brings Internet connections and online teaching materials to a select group of schools, many remote primary schools across the country are still without telephones. Rather than broadening access to education, the incorporation of educational technologies seems to be reproducing existing inequalities.

Especially in poorer societies, there is a marked difference between the private, internationalised sector and the national public sector. Vietnam is the poorest and least technologically developed of the three countries considered in this study, having an average per capita income of just USD200 per annum, which is much lower than Singapore and Malaysia. Vietnam has been connected to the Internet only since November 1997, but its use in education is developing rapidly.

In mid 1999, there were around 30,000 Internet subscribers in Vietnam. To give some indication of the rate of growth, the largest Internet Service Provider, the Vietnam Datacommunication Company, has over 18,000 subscribers, of which 7,733 joined in the first half of 1999.

Significantly, foreigners hold around one third of Internet accounts in Vietnam, while comprising a tiny fraction of the population. Government agencies and business enterprises hold one quarter of all accounts and individuals hold the remainder. Many institutional subscribers have many individual users. At the other end of the spectrum, Singapore has the highest standard of living in South East Asia.

The government of Singapore is looking to make the country a global hub for e-commerce as a way to maintain economic growth in the wake of the Asian financial crisis. The government estimated in 1998 that e-commerce transactions in Singapore would total USD150 million by the end of that year.

In recent years there has been considerable government investment in technology infrastructure. In a recent survey of IT infrastructure investment in 55 countries, Singapore was ranked fourth in the world, behind the United States, Sweden and Finland.

Singapore had 394,000 dial-up Internet subscribers in 1998, or around 10% of the population. Other estimates put total Internet access (dial-up, work and school) at 17 percent of the population in 1998 but these figures are increasing rapidly. In early 2000, the Singapore government announced a three-year initiative intended to make the country one of the top five information societies in the world, in terms of rates of Internet use and home PC ownership.

These will be coordinated by the Infocomm Development Authority and include such measures as providing free e-mail address and Web pages for all citizens over five years of age and distributing 30,000 used computers with software, modems and free Internet access to low-income households.

Such measures are explicitly intended to overcome the digital divide and have the potential to significantly reduce barriers to access for poor students. Singapore has long been using educational technology. Since independence in 1965, educational television has been used to support classroom teaching. In response to the current national IT agenda, the Ministry of Education has developed an IT Masterplan, a comprehensive strategy that aims to integrate information technology throughout the educational system.

The Internet allows for far more constant and ongoing relationships to be established between lecturers and researchers in different countries. In academia, the Internet has become a necessity for inclusion and participation in contemporary global networks.

As the management and production of information becomes ever more central to contemporary capitalism, the divide between inclusion and exclusion in the global flows of information become more crucial.

Many academics in South East Asia are only slowly gaining entry to these networks, as the infrastructure is put in place and as the content of online academic interchange becomes less centred on activities in the United States.

While most academics in Malaysia now have Internet connections, very few academics in Vietnam do, and these tend to be foreign nationals working in transnational institutions or ICT specialists working in computer science departments in public institutions. Universities have always been relatively internationalised workplaces, and many academic staff will have studied or worked in another country at some stage in their career.

In developing countries, it is common for a majority of academics to have received a large part of their education in developed countries. Many of the lecturers in the universities visited were educated in American and British Universities. As one lecturer in a Malaysian university explained, lecturers bring back what they have learnt in these countries and adapt it to local conditions. As well as bringing back knowledge from abroad which is then adapted to local conditions, this experience creates international linkages which the lecturers continue to develop upon their return.

International postgraduate study-Masters and Doctoral programs-which many lecturers in Malaysia, Singapore and Vietnam have experienced, often establishes ongoing research, publishing and teaching connections.

Opportunities for international colleagues to meet face-to-face are infrequent, and in the past, such networks were largely maintained by letter-writing and occasional phone calls. Now, e-mail has allowed these international collaborations to be maintained on a day-to-day basis much more easily. Internet access is helping Vietnamese universities participate in global academic networks. In the past lecturers would bring back suitcases full of books on their return to Vietnam. Now they order books and download articles online.

The IT department subscribes online to The American Computer Magazine and IEEE International Electronic Engineering. They now have faster access to international information technology developments. Staff now obtain international scholarship and grant information online and can apply for these directly.

In past students and academics had to rely on the government to organise these. They have established international relationships with particular lecturers overseas who organise funding and exchanges. At a private transnational provider in Vietnam, like AIT, the communications infrastructure now means that they are as connected to global networks as any other institution in the world. Educational providers must now decide whether they will require their students to provide their own computer and Internet access.

Many universities in the most technologically advanced societies now require their students to provide their own a computer and Internet access, and this is also beginning to be a requirement in private universities in Malaysia. Public distance education providers in South East Asia cannot expect their students to have access to computers and the Internet.

In 1999, Internet access and installation charges were cut by up to 50 percent on 1998 prices. There are different rates for government officials and general users. Two Malaysian private universities that were visited in this study-the International Medical University and UNITAR-are strongly encouraging their students to purchase personal computers.

UNITAR has its own IT shop that sells desktop computers and notebooks at special prices for UNITAR students through a deal between the institution and a manufacturer. The university provides finance so that students can purchase a PC with a small deposit and regular monthly payments. Because UNITAR's viability is reliant on students owning computers, it wants to ensure there are minimal barriers to its students owning PCs.

UNITAR argues that the money students save in commuting costs and lower fees should be put towards purchasing a PC. IMU is also entering into an agreement with a hardware supplier to decrease costs to its students. It is planning to move to a new building in which it will provide numerous Internet access points for notebook computers rather than traditional computer labs. From September 1999, new students must provide their own notebook computer.

UTUM would also like to see their students migrate onto the net, but considers that this is not a realistic expectation of all students in the short term both due to financial constraints and poor telecommunications infrastructure in some places.

Distance education providers such as Universitas Terbuka in Indonesia, Universiti Sains Malaysia and Hanoi Open University have expanded access to higher education for students in outlying areas and for working adults. These institutions are slowly integrating new technologies into teaching and learning, but are hampered by their students' lack of access to computer equipment and because they lack the significant funds required for such innovation.

Meanwhile, new privately-owned entrants into the distance education market such as UNITAR are capitalising on the promise of online education, painting themselves as virtual universities. Distance education can be offered with varying levels of student support. In most cases, printed learning materials and text books are sent to the students.

Increasingly, CD-ROMs, videos and the World Wide Web are being used to supplement these printed resources. When discussing distance education internationally, it is important to distinguish between 'remotely-supported' and 'locally-supported' distance education.

Remotely-supported distance education is delivered to students who study independently and have little face-to-face contact with teaching staff and other students. This is common in Australia and in some other Western countries but rare in South East Asia. Much more common is locally-supported distance education, in which a local study centre provides various services to students, from tutorial support to library facilities. This may involve short-term visits by lecturers or tutors from a central campus or ongoing teaching from locally recruited staff who are able to contextualise centrally-produced teaching materials.

Most transnational distance education providers contract local partners to provide a range of services to students. Increasingly, institutions are providing students with access to tutors via the Internet, using e-mail, discussion forums and on-line tutorials. The Hanoi Open University (HOU) was opened in 1993 as a dual mode university, offering both on-campus and distance education, with the aim of broadening access to tertiary education in Vietnam.

There are currently around 50,000 students enrolled in distance education at university level in Vietnam, most of whom are studying at the HOU, the Ho Chi Minh City Semi-Public Open University or Hue University.

HOU currently has around 32,000 students, of which half are distance students, quarter full-time on-campus students and quarter part-time on-campus students. The language of instruction is Vietnamese. The demographics of distance education in Vietnam are similar to those in other countries.

While most of HOU's full-time students are school-leavers, most distance students are working and many have previous degrees. As a HOU administrator explained, working adults 'want to take distance education so that they can be working and they can be learning at the same time. And, for example, if they are busy this month and they can not take the test or exam, maybe next month or the month after next they will come for the test or the examination again.'

HOU has 12 local study centres across Vietnam for distance students, who are located all over the country, including remote and mountainous areas. Tutors and lecturers visit these at regular times to conduct tutorials, revision classes, tests and examinations in conjunction with teachers based at the local study centre.

HOU allows students to study without attending the local study centres but few do in practice. Teaching materials are mostly in printed form, supplemented by video and audio tapes, television and radio programs. HOU plans to put computers in use for distance education and has developed its own Intranet, which it plans to put to use for distance education.

In a technical sense, relying on Internet-based communication allows the institution to operate globally. In the earlier print/post phase of remotely-supported distance education, most students tended to live near the institution, and almost entirely within the same country.

Internationalisation was difficult due to the cost, slowness and unreliability of international communications. By using e-mail and the Web, it is now possible for prospective students to choose from a wide range of courses offered by providers based in many different nations.

A number of online universities have begun to market themselves internationally, including Jones

International and the University of Southern Queensland. Two institutions in the countries visited refer to themselves as virtual universities. The differences between them offer some indication of the ways in which this organisational form may be applied in South East Asia.

In the past, universities saw themselves as a place apart, to quote the title of a recent history of the University of Melbourne. They strived to maintain and develop bodies of knowledge developed in Europe's elite institutions by operating independently, disembedded from their local contexts.

In this sense, both the form and content of modern higher education has always been international to some extent, however in a very different form to the globalisation that has occurred in the latter half of the twentieth century. Universities have long seen science and technology as universal, culturally neutral forms of knowledge. These disciplines have been taught globally with little regard for local differences.

Through the spread of Western education around the world, these forms of knowledge have become globally dominant while local knowledge, skills and cultures are often overlooked. Some writers draw attention to the ways in which the dominant forms of Western science have appropriated elements of knowledge systems from around the globe and combined them to develop a coherent world-view.

In this way, science can be de-Westernised, and made more relevant to non-Western students by teaching about the diverse cultural roots of science. This does not seem to be occurring widely in practice, and the tendency is more commonly for local knowledges to be treated as inferior to bodies of knowledge imported from the most technologically advanced post-industrial societies. While science and technology education are perhaps the most globalised, the internationalisation of other disciplines is also occurring.

The more the process of economic globalization deepens, the more the inter-penetration of networks of production and management expands across borders, and the closer become the links between the conditions of the labor force in different countries, placed at different levels of wages and social protection, but decreasingly distinct in terms of skills and technology.' The most internationally adaptable areas are those characterised by 'skills and concepts which are readily translatable across countries and cultures, a strong vocational emphasis, high student and/or industry demand for tailored and flexibly delivered programs and strong industry pressure for standardisation of content across institutions.'

Role of internet in Transnational Education

The Internet is now essential to the operation of offshore campuses and other forms of transnational education such as international distance education. The three offshore educators visited in this study-Asian Institute of Technology Centre in Vietnam, Monash University Malaysia and TMC Educational Group, Singapore-all used Internet-based communication as their primary means of integrating their campus and their students into an international organisation. All three providers deliver courses through a combination of face-to-face teaching and technologically mediated materials.

Transnational courses are sometimes tailored to local conditions as required, but usually only minimal modifications are made, mainly in terms of content and assignment questions.

International education providers increasingly need to bridge the divide between globally- and locally-relevant education. Employers around the world now look for graduates with a balance of universal and specific knowledge, who understand local conditions but are able to work in internationalised contexts. The Asian Institute of Technology (AIT) is an international institution based in Bangkok. It was established over 40 as the South East Asian Treaty Organisation Graduate School of Engineering to serve the educational needs of the South East Asian region and it continues to be funded by many governments and foundations. It now has faculty from more than 25 countries and students from more than 40 countries.

AIT has two centres in Vietnam. The AIT Centre Vietnam, located in Hanoi, was established in 1993, as the institution's first branch outside Bangkok. It provides postgraduate education, short-term training courses, language training. Vietnamese students constitute the largest group of foreign students at AIT in Bangkok. Many educational commentators in Britain, North America and Australia see the use of technology as leading to a more student-centred learning environment.

A student's ability to engage in technologically-mediated communication requires an understanding of the cultural conventions of the medium. People have to learn how to use the telephone-how to talk to an unseen other, how to adopt a 'telephone' voice appropriate to the type of conversation being engaged in and how to gauge meanings in the absence of visual cues. Likewise, e-mail correspondence has a different etiquette to letter writing and synchronous chat discussions operate differently to face-to-face group discussions.

In all societies, students may find communicating online just as intimidating as in person. One lecturer with considerable experience teaching mixed groups comprising Australian and South East Asia students in both face-to-face and online discussion forums had come to the conclusion that South East Asian students 'were much more active if they felt secure in the online environment and they would talk in ways they would never do in class.'

5

Skill Development in Education

The intent of knowledge and skill-based pay is to supplement or replace the traditional schedule with a pay system that motivates teachers to acquire and demonstrate the application of knowledge and skills that more directly contribute to better school performance and student achievement. The importance of seniority as a basis for pay is reduced or even eliminated.

While knowledge and skill-based pay programs also reward individual teachers, the reward is based on demonstrating knowledge and skills with respect to public, relatively detailed standards or descriptions of practice. These standards both guide assessor judgments and make known to teachers 'up front' what they need to do to demonstrate the knowledge and skills. Since any teacher who demonstrates the skills receives the reward, teachers do not compete for a share of a fixed fund or merit pay pool.

These features of knowledge and skill-based pay may make it more effective in motivating more teachers than merit pay. Because knowledge and skill-based pay programs are new and quite rare in the K-12 sector, it is not yet possible to obtain definitive evidence about the success of these programs in influencing instructional capacity or in improving student achievement. Knowledge and skill-based pay systems have the potential to positively impact instructional capacity, and in turn student achievement, in three ways.

i) They provide incentives for teachers to develop specific knowledge and skills needed to increase instructional capacity. More highly skilled teachers, in turn, have the capacity to deliver higher quality instruction, which, when combined with motivation to improve instruction and a context conducive to applying the skills, should lead to improved instruction.

ii) Allocating higher pay to teachers who have these skills, these programs should help attract and retain high capacity teachers, and by denying higher pay to teachers without the skills, discourage lower capacity teachers from staying. Over time, the average skill level of a faculty should increase, improving the average quality of instruction.

iii) A well-developed knowledge and skill-based pay systems rests on a model of competence that can also be used in teacher evaluation, professional development, and even recruitment and selection.

Acquiring and demonstrating the skills must also have consequences teachers value. While it is safe to assume teachers value pay increases, these rewards also must be large enough to be perceived as worth the effort expended to acquire the specified skills. These rewards will also be more motivating if the knowledge and skill model on which the program is based is accepted by teachers as consistent with their conceptions of quality instruction and a highly-skilled teacher.

Presumably, most teachers want to consider themselves good at what they do and are interested in developing their skills toward their ideal of a highly-skilled teacher. They may find this process of development intrinsically rewarding. The extrinsic and intrinsic rewards work against each other. It is likely that the extrinsic pay reward will have a more motivating effect if it is consistent with the intrinsic reward.

This means that the knowledge and skill model needs to be consistent with teachers' beliefs about what constitutes of a highly-skilled teacher. Finally, teachers may also value avoiding certain negative consequences, such as not being recognized as highly- skilled or expert. Alternatively, adoption of new forms of teacher compensation by pioneer organisations may be motivated by the desire to appear innovative or by the desire of influential decision makers to implement strongly-held ideas about which teachers should be paid more.

In addition, a pay system change can present an opportunity to further other agendas, such as providing additional pay for all teachers or assuring the public that teacher pay is related to teacher performance. The motivation for moving to knowledge and skill-based pay is important, because it is likely to be related to design features such as the knowledge and skills in the model and the extent to which the new pay structure departs from the traditional salary schedule.

One might expect that where the primary motivation is to improve student achievement, the knowledge and skill model will focus on instruction, and pay increases for developing instructional skills will be greater. One form of teacher participation is through collective bargaining. However, it may be difficult to design a knowledge and skill-based pay program through the standard adversarial collective bargaining process of proposal and counter-proposal, with each side seeking maximum advantage.

Knowledge and skill-based pay programs require a coherent design based on some agreed-upon conception of good teaching. Many technical details, such as how knowledge and skills will be assessed, need to be addressed. So it is expected that these programs would be designed either outside the formal contract negotiation process or though an interest-based process that focuses the parties' attention on mutual goals.

Another important aspect of the design process is how program designers decide what knowledge and skills to reward. Designers in the private sector appear to have used inductive, deductive, or adaptive approaches. The inductive approach involves using job analysis or relying on research to identify those knowledge and skills likely to contribute to employee performance. One version of this method is to study known good and average performers to find out what knowledge and skills differ between these groups.

The deductive approach involves starting from the organization's strategy, then trying to identify the knowledge and skill employees need to carry it out. The adaptive approach involves starting with a knowledge and skill model developed elsewhere, then changing it to fit local goals and conditions.

Though the use of the adaptive method in the private sector has been criticized because it does not provide a unique source of competitive advantage, it avoids reinventing the wheel, especially for those core knowledge and skills likely to be common across organizations. In the K-12 sector the core technology of instruction is similar across schools.

Since there is currently little competition among schools, there is little incentive for very different specifications of knowledge and skills to be identified. At the heart of a knowledge and skill-based pay program is the specification of the knowledge and skills teachers will be rewarded for developing. The theory of action assumes that the knowledge and skills specified will be those teachers need to deliver instruction that contributes directly to student achievement.

Thus an important facet of this dimension is the degree to which the knowledge and skills rewarded are related to instruction. Another important facet is the extent to which the knowledge and skills rewarded are organized into an integrated model with a defined continuum of skills or expertise.

Knowledge and skill-based pay programs in the private sector often structure the knowledge and skills rewarded into a set of career levels, levels defined by rating scales or sequences of skills to be mastered. A number of different structures of knowledge and skills representing a progression from entry level to accomplished teaching.

Such a structure could provide a roadmap for teachers seeking to develop their knowledge and skills as well as convenient attachment points for pay increases. It could also be used to align other parts of the human resource management system, especially professional development programs, and as a guide for teachers working to develop mastery of quality instruction. The traditional degrees and credits seem to be viewed as fair by teachers, but they may not have high validity as indicators of whether skills can be applied in the classroom.

Properly constructed and administered, performance-based assessments, which function as samples of teachers' instruction, have the potential to ensure that the skills can be applied and to be perceived as valid and fair, due to their close connection with practice. Thus one facet of this dimension is the extent to which performance-based assessments are used, rather than degrees and credits, to provide evidence of knowledge and skill acquisition.

External assessments could be used in combination with local assessments to maintain the rigor of the system. The teacher performance evaluation literature suggests that local assessors such as principals face many incentives to be less than rigorous.

If almost all teachers are judged to have the skills, due to leniency of local assessors, the contingency between skill acquisition and receiving the reward the motivational model postulates as necessary is reduced. The theory of action proposes that the extra pay offered will motivate teachers to acquire the knowledge and skills needed to improve instruction.

To motivate, the pay incentive provided must be valued. Experience with the traditional salary schedule suggests that teachers value pay rewards enough to collect years of seniority, credits, and degrees. But to motivate the acquisition of the new, possibly hard-to-master skills needed to improve instruction, the incentives must be of sufficient size to attract teachers attention and to be perceived as commensurate with the effort needed to acquire the skills. It is reasonable to expect that the greater the size of the incentive, the more motivational effect, all else equal.

So an important facet of this dimension is the size of the incentive offered. To the extent that knowledge and skill rewards replace the traditional pay increases for seniority and educational attainment, we might expect teachers to be more motivated to attain the skills, since the traditional opportunities for pay increases have been reduced. A more radical change in the pay structure, de-emphasizing seniority and educational attainment unrelated to classroom instruction, sends a stronger signal that new knowledge and skills are needed.

Knowledge and skill pay programs might be located on a continuum ranging from those that supplement the traditional salary schedule by simply adding additional pay opportunities based on knowledge and skill acquisition, to complete replacement of the traditional schedule's seniority steps and educational attainment lanes with a set of pay levels based only on knowledge and skill attainment.

One might expect that the greater the perceived need to improve instruction, the more the traditional salary schedule would be modified and the larger the incentives for knowledge and skill acquisition would be. A knowledge and skill-based pay system carries risks for teachers accustomed to automatic pay increases based on seniority.

It may be particularly unattractive to more senior teachers because it places less emphasis on seniority as a criterion for pay differentiation, and can require developing new skills, which may not be as good an investment of effort for them. To get a knowledge and skill-based pay program accepted may require some provision that compensates teachers in some way for the increased risk or reduces the threat that the emphasis on new skills can represent to senior teachers.

Thus another feature of interest is whether the programs include provisions intended to make the new system acceptable to potential opponents such as veteran teachers. While knowledge and skill-based pay offers substantial benefits, it is also likely to require additional investments, including the costs of increased professional development and additional administrative overhead as well as of higher salaries.

Private sector experience with knowledge and skill-based pay programs suggests that administrative costs increase and per-employee salary costs increase. Individual pay increases are thought to be offset by increases in productivity and greater flexibility in staff utilization due to cross-training.

The knowledge and skills are not those that allow teachers to do more different jobs, therefore allowing elimination of support staff. Therefore in the long run we would expect higher costs, which need to be funded by new money or reallocation of existing resources. In 1999s, one-third of teachers reported feeling very well or well prepared to use computers and the Internet for instruction, with less experienced teachers indicating they felt more prepared to use technology than their more experienced colleagues. For many instructional activities, teachers who reported feeling well prepared or very well prepared to use technology were more likely to use it or assign students to use it than teachers who reported feeling unprepared.

Whereas half of all teachers reported that college and graduate work prepared them to use technology, less experienced teachers were generally much more likely than their more experienced colleagues to indicate that this education prepared them to use computers and the Internet. Most teachers indicated that professional development activities on a number of topics were available to them, including training on software applications, the use of the Internet, and the use of computers and basic computer training.

The 1999 teacher survey of technology use asked a number of questions about professional development availability and participation. Teachers reported that professional development training on the use of computers and basic computer training was the type most likely to be available to them, followed by software applications, use of the Internet, and integration of technology into the curriculum and classroom instruction.

Teachers' use of computers or the Internet at school varied for some types of uses by school poverty level (the percentage of students in the school eligible for free or reduced-price lunches). Teachers in schools with a school poverty level of less than 11 percent were more likely to use computers or the Internet "a lot" for creating instructional materials than teachers in schools with a school poverty level of 71 percent or more. This pattern also held for teachers who used computers for administrative record keeping.

Sixty-six percent of public school teachers reported using computers or the Internet for instruction during class time. Forty-one percent of teachers reported assigning students work that involved computer applications such as word processing and spreadsheets to a moderate or large extent; 31 percent of teachers reported assigning practice drills and 30 percent reported assigning research using the Internet to a moderate or large extent.

The ways teachers direct students to use computers or the Internet varied by instructional level, main teaching assignment, and the school poverty level. Elementary school teachers were more likely than secondary school teachers to assign students practice drills using computers and to have their students use computers or the Internet to solve problems.

Secondary school teachers, however, were more likely to assign research using the Internet. Teachers in the lowest poverty schools were more likely to report assigning students work involving computer applications, research using CD-ROMs, and research using the Internet to a moderate or large extent than teachers in the highest poverty schools.

There is an important relationship between state-mandated testing and teachers' beliefs and practice. At the same time the state testing does matter by influencing what teachers say and do, so, too, do other things, such as teachers' knowledge of subject matter, their approaches to teaching, their views of learning, and the amalgam of experience and status they possess in the school organisation.

Consequently, although a relationship between the state-mandated testing and teachers' beliefs and practice does exist, testing does not appear to be an exclusive or a primary lever of change. In the United States, state-mandated testing programs reportedly tied to new or revised state curriculum standards are currently being developed and used in a majority of states.

Over the past decade, of the 48 states that have statewide assessment programs, almost all report having revamped or being in the process of revamping their state tests to align them more closely with some or all of the specific state standards.

One important assumption underlying some of the recent changes made in state-mandated testing is "that testing drives much of what teachers do, and so curricular and instructional change will occur if and when the tests change". Some of the recent changes made in state-level assessments involves increasing the "power" or "stakes" of these tests through the use of rewards and sanctions.

A low-stakes test has no significant, tangible, or direct consequences attached to the results, with information alone assumed to be a sufficient incentive for people to act. The theory behind this policy is that a standardised test can reliably and validly measure student achievement; that politicians, educators, parents, and the public will then act on the information generated by the test; and that actions based on tests results will improve educational quality and student achievement.

In the past, state policymakers have typically relied upon low-stakes state-mandated testing to address a number of goals. In a profile of state-mandated testing programs in 1992-93, the most prevalent purposes of state programs were accountability, instructional improvement, and program evaluation.

With the arrival of standards-based reform and the explicit setting of standards that define what teachers should teach and students should learn, a greater role for state-mandated testing has emerged. In sixty years of vast international research on school testing, the policy of emphasising test performance in order to improve education has never been validated.

The increased use of state-mandated testing as a lever for change has not been paralleled by significant growth in knowledge about how testing affects teaching, learning, and schools in actual practice. The idea that state-mandated testing will somehow lead to better teaching and learning expresses more hope than reality.

While state-mandated testing did appear to inspire "changes" occurring at the local level in both states, those changes to be "merely differences" rather than "changes for the better" or improvements. The existence of a relationship between state-mandated testing and teacher beliefs and practice is consistently confirmed. State-mandated tests do matter and do influence what teachers say and do in their classrooms.

But while there is overall agreement that a relationship between the two does exist, the nature of that relationship is neither simple nor easy and requires further elucidation. The state-mandated testing has had significant influence on teachers' beliefs and practice. Teachers perceived the state tests as having a mostly negative impact on their beliefs and practice, whereas others said teachers perceived the state tests to be a mixed bag

Today, several countries faced ballot initiatives that propose to functionally eliminate bilingual education in favor of English-only approaches. Education policy concerning the instruction of limited English proficient (LEP) students in the United States has been debated for a number of decades and considerable attention has been given to the best method of instruction for these students.

In recent years, the controversy regarding how to best educate LEP students has surfaced in the form of political legislation.

According to the United States Department of Education the term "limited English proficient" refers to individuals who were not born in the U. S. and whose native language is other than English, or come from environments in which a language other than English is dominant.

Bilingual education programs provide a substantial amount of content area instruction in the students' native language, while some time each day is spent developing English skills. It should be noted, however, that the actual implementation of programs varies across states, districts, schools, and even classrooms. Proponents of bilingual education argue that without support in their native language, LEP students will fall behind academically while they are learning English.

Proponents of English immersion argue that instructional time devoted to intensive learning of English will more likely benefit children's academic achievement in a second language environment. Recently, the debate surrounding the education of LEP students has shifted to the political arena.

Over the past two decades, many educational reformers, particularly those associated with the standards movement, hold that the key to improving student performance lies in improving the schools. If academic standards are rigorous, curriculum and assessments are aligned to those standards, and teachers possess the skills to teach at the level the standards demand, student performance will improve. However, this perspective is to some extent at odds with another that has emerged from the discussion about school improvement, namely that it is students rather than schools that make the difference.

The social backgrounds of students that play the key role in their ability to learn, and only by moving outside of the educational system and attacking the pervasive economic inequalities that exist in the U.S. can student performance be improved. The US' National Assessment of Educational Progress (NAEP), which includes a comprehensive set of classroom practices along with student test scores and other characteristics of students and teachers. The statistical technique of multilevel structural equation modeling (MSEM) is employed to address the major methodological shortcomings of the quantitative literature, namely the failure to distinguish between school- and student-level effects, to measure relationships among independent variables, and to explicitly model measurement error.

Status of Education

The majority of developing countries have already set up appropriate institutional bodies and mechanisms for the preparation and monitoring of education plans conducive to the implementation of the EFA Goals. Of the 66 countries responding, 45 (68%) that they had already set up EFA forums or EFA-related bodies, while 21 (32%) that they had not yet done so. Results show that in most countries there is already an Education Development Plan (EDP). Forty-one countries of the 66 countries responding reported having a plan (62%), with 18 countries (27%) saying that their plan is being prepared.

Only seven nations (11%) having a plan. Thirty-nine of the 41 plans were prepared before the Dakar Forum, in some cases more than 10 years before. One serious progress towards EFA is the lack of information on how many countries have included teachers' unions, NGOs and other representatives of civil society in their planning processes.

In evaluating progress, it is important to determine not only the extent to which governments have sought the co-operation of civil society in drafting their plans, but also whether they have sought out representatives of the most important stakeholders outside of government.

Developing a mechanism to monitor co-operation with civil society should be a priority in future data gathering. At least 48 of the 66 countries do not seem to have reliable capacities for data collection, processing and/or analysis for preparing EFA action plans. Moreover, in the majority of countries, education information systems, which are prerequisites for providing necessary data and information for EFA. Most developing countries said that they would require methodological and technical support for the preparation of the EFA plans or the strengthening of existing plans.

Specifically, 55 (83%) of responding countries indicated that they needed support, while only 7 (11%) said that no support was needed. Four countries (6%) did not respond to this question. To sum up, it is clear that most countries need to revisit their existing plans or to develop them in accordance with the EFA criteria. And most need help in doing so. A serious strategy for co-operation should be thought out and worked out urgently in order for agencies to provide the required technical and financial support for preparation and adjustment of the plans.

This strategy should be based on the respective comparative advantages and capabilities of partner agencies—national, regional and global —with a view to increasing the effectiveness and efficiency of the support. This assistance must take two forms: technical support and financial assistance.

Under UNESCO leadership, a number of EFA mechanisms are being set up to co-ordinate the identification of needs, fund-raising, assistance to countries in the development of national action plans, capacity-building of ministries of education and so forth. By all accounts the 46 nations of sub-Saharan Africa face some of the greatest challenges in meeting the goals of EFA. Problems such as widespread poverty, the pressures of population growth and heavy debt burdens have been compounded by issues such as political instability, armed conflicts and the HIV/AIDS pandemic.

Countries in the region have committed themselves to working both co-operatively among themselves and through a variety of partnerships to achieve the goals of EFA. Forty-five of the 46 countries have nominated national EFA co-ordinators, and they have pledged to 'mobilize all stakeholders, partners and governments' to ensure that each country has completed a national plan of action by September 2002.

The plan calls for a regional synthesis to be endorsed politically by African ministers of education in December 2002. A participatory EFA Regional Action Plan has been drafted and reviewed with the help of numerous EFA sponsors. Regional networking and consultations have been conducted with NGOs, bilateral and multilateral partners, and some regional memos of understanding have been drawn up with various United Nations agencies related to the mobilization of resources.

The UNESCO regional office in Dakar, Senegal (BREDA) has participated in many national, regional and international meetings and has established a regional experts roster. Technical support has also been forthcoming for the preparation of national plans of action. Improvement of the quality of education is a priority in most Arab States, and most of the twenty countries in the region initiated education reforms during the 1990s.

At least half of them have identified EFA as a focal point for such reforms and established some sort of EFA Forum. In a number of cases, existing reform plans are being updated so as to embrace EFA targets in general and the goals and strategies of the Dakar Framework in particular. Many Arab states have identified enhanced education of girls and the promotion of early childhood care and education as two important priority areas for their socioeconomic development.

Countries in the region articulate the need for financial support, including debt relief or debt reduction, if they are to carry out their commitment to EFA. The most vigorous regional activities in support of EFA have been in South-East/East Asia, where a sub-regional forum has been formed with many bilateral and multilateral partners. Annual meetings have been held of national EFA co-ordinators in collaboration with a United Nations Economic and Social Commission for Asia and the Pacific, ESCAP Technical Working Group on EFA.

Most countries in the sub-region have refined existing basic education plans, with some ensuring strong linkages with sector-wide plans. Comprehensive planning mechanisms and procedures are in place in most countries, though often without national forums or widespread involvement of civil society. The creation of the sub-regional forum was mandated at a ministerial meeting in April 2001. Draft NAPs were presented by all countries at the ministerial meeting in April, but found inadequate NGO involvement or lack of active participation of major EFA partners.

Most of the countries have formed a Technical Support Group for EFA and the formation of a Regional Forum of EFA for the South Asian countries is expected. Pakistan was selected to host the next ministerial meeting of South Asia in 2003. Sub-regional activities are being developed in curriculum development and learning achievement, monitoring of EFA progress and non-formal education. National EFA roundtables have been held in most countries of Central Asia/Caucasus, and a revolving EFA Forum of five countries is scheduled to be established in October.

Sub-regional and national meetings have been organized on monitoring of learning achievement, reaching the unreached, non-formal education, AIDS and other topics. Collaboration has been close with UNICEF and national and international NGOs. National action plans have been completed in thirteen countries in the Pacific. These have been facilitated by a strong sense of regional identity and co-operation, but there is inadequate involvement of the full range of EFA partners.

Governments are now awaiting the support promised in the Dakar Framework for Action. There has been an increased desire of NGOs and civil society organizations in the Asia and Pacific region to become involved in EFA, but this has not always been met by government encouragement. Genuine encouragement in

EFA planning is dependent on strong donor commitment, but much has been done in the Philippines, however, not only by donors but also by civil society organizations including NGOs.

At the dawn of the new century 875 million of the world 's citizens are illiterate. One out of every five children aged 6-11 in developing countries -an estimated 113 million -is not in school, 60 per cent of them are girls. Nine countries -Bangladesh, Brazil, China, Egypt, India, Indonesia, Mexico, Nigeria and Pakistan (E9)- are home to 70 per cent of the world 's illiterates. In South Asia an estimated 60 per cent of women are illiterate.

Worldwide, one woman in four cannot read. In South Asia and sub-Saharan Africa, less than three out of four pupils reach Grade 5. The HIV/AIDS pandemic threatens to wipe out much of the progress made in boosting literacy and general education levels. Up to 10 per cent of teachers are expected to die in the worst-affected African countries. The World Conference on Education for All placed basic education high on the development agenda.

Since then real progress has been made: 10 million more children attend school each year and adult literacy rates rose to 85 per cent for men and 74 per cent for women. Strong political commitment can make the dream of Education for All (EFA) a reality.

Many countries -not only in the richest parts of the world but also in Latin America, the Caribbean, East Asia and even in Africa -are now approaching universal primary education for the first time. Countries such as Botswana, Brazil, China, Mexico, Sri Lanka and Tunisia are showing the way.

In April 2000, more than 1,100 delegates from 164 countries reaffirmed their commitment to EFA at the World Education Forum in Dakar, Senegal. They adopted the Dakar Framework for Action -a bold, practical document laying out goals and strategies for achieving Education for All. The six Dakar goals:

i) Expand early childhood care and education.

ii) Free and compulsory education of good quality by 2015.

iii) Promote the acquisition of life-skills by adolescents and youth.

iv) Expand adult literacy by 50 per cent by 2015.

v) Eliminate gender disparities by 2005 and achieve gender equality in education by 2015.

vi) Enhance educational quality.

Education for All is the responsibility and prerogative of countries. They are responsible for mobilizing efforts and additional resources and must secure the involvement of all stakeholders. Their determination is key to the success of the EFA drive. Non-governmental organizations, teacher unions, religious organizations, parents and learners play a major role in education as they work with communities in providing alternative solutions where state provision is absent or insufficient.

They have the advantage of being flexible, more innovative and closer to the grassroots and local cultures. Bilateral and multilateral development agencies are supporting countries 'action through technical assistance, funding support, enhanced monitoring of EFA progress, greater co-ordination of efforts and strengthened partnerships between governments and civil society. UNESCO 's Director-General convenes annually a high-level, small and flexible group to sustain political momentum and mobilize resources for basic education.

UNESCO also brings together an EFA working group of experts to receive technical guidance, build and sustain partnerships and support regional and sub-regional networks. An EFA Observatory has been set up within the UNESCO Institute for Statistics to monitor progress towards EFA.

New indicators are being developed and countries receive assistance in collecting educational statistics. Making Education for All a reality is affordable: the cost of providing the world 's children with primary education by 2015 will require between $8 billion and $15 billion extra spending a year -less than 2 per cent of the annual estimated military costs worldwide.

Most of the money will come from the countries themselves, through changing priorities and adopting cost-effective measures. A new global initiative is seeking to ensure more effective donor co-ordination and increased aid to basic education, in particular through accelerated debt relief. This goal will remain a distant dream unless a major effort is undertaken to accelerate the current trends.

Primary schools in developing countries will need to accommodate about 156 million more children than in 1997, an increase of 27 per cent. At a minimum, this will require maintaining the previous enrolment effort. A particular effort will be needed in sub-Saharan Africa, which will have to find 88 million additional school places. South Asia will have to enrol about 40 million more children an increase of one third -requiring at least the same pace of effort as in the 1990s. Africa and South Asia face substantial challenges, in particular in the least developed countries, where success will require more than a doubling of past efforts.

Some regions of the world, notably East Asia, the Pacific, Latin America and the Caribbean will reach the goal by maintaining nearly the same level of effort as in the past decade. Urgent action is needed in countries in crisis and with high HIV/AIDS infection if the EFA goals are to be reached. Fifty countries around the world are in situations of emergency, caused by armed conflict, chronic crisis or natural disasters. United Nations agencies are working with bilateral donors and civil society on inter-agency flagship programmes to accelerate efforts, by co-ordinating action, providing technical assistance and developing knowledge and experience to put these countries on track.

The achievement of EFA goals in Poverty Reduction Strategy Papers (PRSPs) is analysed, and a preliminary assessment is provided on the scope and the nature of the engagement of civil society in planning, given its importance as an indicator of national commitment to EFA.

The World Education Forum underscored the urgency of developing ways of mitigating the impact of HIV/AIDS on education and developing education strategies to combat the pandemic. It also recognized that countries in conflict or facing reconstruction require special attention. Planning for HIV/AIDS—will examine the development of planning that is responsive to the circumstances of people who live with HIV/AIDS, and to those who survive in the face of crisis, conflict and emergency.

Since Dakar, the concept of a credible plan has been closely associated with the commitment in the Framework for Action, that no countries seriously committed to education for all will be thwarted in their achievement of this goal by a lack of resources. The underlying principles and goals of EFA were set in Jomtien. They were reaffirmed and expanded in Dakar where there was the opportunity to draw on a broad spectrum of comparative educational knowledge and experience.

Children excluded from school, girls education and the participation of disabled learners were among the issues discussed. Community partnerships in education and the role of non-governmental organizations, school health and nutrition, literacy and education, early childhood c re and development and the application of new technologies for education also received attention.

Internationally, there is an enormous fund of knowledge and comparative experience on how to provide good quality education for young children, how to promote gender equality, and how to reach the poor and the excluded. This knowledge is not always shared or well communicated but it exists.

However, in many respects, Dakar is of political rather than technical and professional significance. It will be judged less by the soundness of its technical debates, and much more by the extent to which it promotes commitment and mobilizes human and financial resources in support of the strategies agreed at the World Education Forum. The realisation of Education For All requires sustained political support, realistic choices about the allocation of scarce resources, and an environment that enables people to engage in an inclusive process of making plans and taking decisions.

In some countries, the plans are a restatement or reformulation of existing plans. And the extent is to which there engagement with civil society that goes beyond set-piece consultation has not always been well defined. If a broader and wider interpretation of planning for EFA is used, wherein countries are revisiting their goals and targets for EFA, building on existing sector strategies and plans, and promoting EFA in other planning processes such as PRSPs, then there is a much stronger case to be made for a larger group of countries.

UNESCO has been the leader in promoting the Dakar commitment to develop EFA National Action Plans and it is the main repository of progress reports, through its Paris headquarters and Regional Bureaux. But as yet, there is no authoritative global analysis that draws on detailed country studies. As a consequence, it is difficult to assess with any degree of confidence, how national governments have interpreted the Dakar planning commitment. Data that are available at the international level are limited, uneven and sometimes difficult to interpret.

Nevertheless, reports from UNESCO's Regional Bureaux highlight a range of education sector planning activities and a considerable variety of interpretations regarding the call for comprehensive EFA National Action Plan by 2002. There are some exceptions to this, however, as the creation of sub-regional forums for the Nordic and Baltic countries and for three Caucasus states demonstrates.

Based on a questionnaire survey carried out in June 2002, UNESCO headquarters has collected data on EFA-related planning activities in fifty-four countries (ten from sub-Saharan Africa, eleven Arab States, thirteen from Asia and the Pacific, fourteen from Latin America and six from Europe). These data suggest that 70% of the countries have set up EFA Forums. They also suggest that 75% of the sample countries are engaged in planning processes that encompass some or all of the Dakar goals, whether in the form of a separate and distinct National EFA Plan or within broader planning frameworks such as education sector plans and national development strategies. The survey records some of the difficulties that confront education sector planners: the lack of reliable data, inadequate technical skills for policy formulation and planning, the absence of robust analyses on costs and the financing of EFA, and the associated difficulty of developing reliable budget projections.

UNESCO's Regional Bureaux have conducted their own surveys of planning for EFA. These provide headline information on the status of plan development, difficulties that are being experienced and the existence of related planning documents and frameworks. In the draft EFA Plan, it is estimated that the Government can fund 40% of an enlarged budget but that external funding will be required to fill the financing gap.

The EFA Plan makes specific reference to the Dakar commitment that no countries seriously committed to Education for All will be thwarted in their achievement by a lack of resources. India's Plan of Action will be finalized by the end of 2002. It will reflect and complement the Sarv Shiksa Abhiyan programme for Universal Elementary Education (UEE) that is designed to ensure that all children aged 6 to 14 will receive eight years of quality education by 2010, as well as India's 10th Five-year Plan 2002 -2007, which includes literacy strategies as well as UEE.

An assessment of Sri Lanka's interpretation of the Dakar commitment, arguing that Sri Lanka has a portfolio of plans. In the Latin America and the Caribbean region there are forty-one countries. In Cuba, it is expected that an EFA Plan will be completed in 2002 to complement the existing 15-year national plan of action. The Dominican Republic and Ecuador both indicate that new EFA plans should be ready by the end of 2002.

In the Caribbean, all countries report existing policies and plans that address EFA goals. Dominic reports that its 1999 Education Development Plan, revised in 2002, addresses EFA objectives. For the forty-six countries that comprise the sub-Saharan Africa region, detailed analysis is limited. Eleven countries are recorded as having EFA plans due for completion by the end of 2002. Other countries are developing their existing sector plans.

The International Strategy to Put the Dakar Framework for Action on Education for All into Operation states that by March 2002, around seventy countries had developed plans for Education for All, although the evidence base for this assertion is not provided. Clearly there is currently some rethinking and modification taking place regarding education plans and strategies tailored to reflect the strengths of existing policies and plans as well as the relevance of the EFA goals to national circumstance.

For example, the government of Democratic People's Republic of Korea is focusing on life skills and the quality of education in the belief that it has met the other goals. There is evidence too of the establishment of EFA Forums and committees even if a new and/or formal

EFA plan is not being constructed, although data on the roles, composition and work of these forums are not readily available.

For the future, if there is to be an effective monitoring process at the regional and international level, there is a clear need for comprehensive database on country-level legislation, policies and plans. This is a matter that UNESCO, its specialized institutes, and other international organizations should address. It is a development with which the Global Report is well placed to assist. In advance of the availability of such a resource, the EFA Global Monitoring Report undertook two exercises.

The Dakar Framework for Action states that national plans: will address problems associated with the chronic under-financing of basic education by establishing budget priorities that reflect a commitment to achieving EFA goals and targets at the earliest possible date, and no later than 2015.

6

Educational Challenges in Globalising World

Knowledge today has become so diversified that it is no longer possible for a serious academic unit to claim that it can cover all components of a specific field of study and offer its students all areas of micro-specialization found in a given area of knowledge.

However, there are now grounds to believe that one major effect of the globalisation phenomenon has been to transform the relations between states into just one system among many other systems of relations created by other globalisation actors, be they business concerns, social movements, cultural organizations, institutions, etc. To sum up, if the interpretation of inter-state relations alone is no longer sufficient for understanding today's world, we must nonetheless admit that these relations are as important as ever.

In fact, globalisation simply means a new space in which other social relations are organized and important dimensions of our lives in society are structured but it has not brought about the disappearance of international relations.

One of the most valuable contributions by academia to the life of our societies is that it constitutes one of the only social spaces in which a critical understanding of phenomena and the search for the truth can be conducted. In this sense, academia is first and foremost a space for dialogue that is essential to our societies and its contribution to the public sphere is unique owing to the quality and originality of the projects, analyses and research that are conducted there It should be noted, however, that any discussion on globalisation today is a delicate undertaking because the word itself has numerous meanings, including many negative connotations that would suggest that common sense has been blacklisted, judgement declared out of bounds and reason set aside.

In a nutshell, it is an issue that polarizes reductive analyzes to extremes and while this is not an original solution, it can, despite everything, prove to be quite useful socially.

To summarize the process, this conceptualization, as it has evolved over more than a century of social sciences and humanities, is based upon well-known reflexes for understanding reality. Our usual way of understanding reality involves cutting it into national portions. In each portion we find a political community—a people, a nation-living on a territory separated from that of its neighbours by clearly defined borders.

This community constructs and reproduces itself through its own internal dynamics. At the heart of this self-propelled construction is the State, an omnipresent architect of social order where it alone is empowered to legislate and enforce the law. The State acts as a modernizing force driving society because it is the most powerful organization and the only sovereign power over the territory. Nonetheless, social sciences and political science in particular have not neglected the outside world.

The division of labour within the discipline has seen the field of international relations take charge of studying the relationships and exchanges that these territorialized communities carry on amongst each other. Except that here, once again, the State is omnipresent in that the political universe made up of international relations is essentially structured by inter-state relations.

The cultural, economic, educational, consumption, intellectual, religious, media, sports and social practices in their everyday lives are a part of social networks that do not share the same socio-spatial demarcation. These networks may be local, national, continental, occidental or even planetary or global. Basically, this theoretical conceptualization assumes, on the one hand, a spatial correspondence between all the components of life in society, namely the economic, cultural, social and political element, and on the other, a territorialized concept of the community that inserts individuals, groups and social classes into a clearly delimited societal framework, one which postulates that the territory contains the life of the society.

In the world of higher education, this social conceptualization is traditionally reflected in national university systems that contain university campuses which are territorialized premises. Thus, it is postulated that the campus contains the academic life since the professor remains the primary agent for teaching and the classroom, the main place for dispensing knowledge. Knowledge is being depersonalized, deterritorialized and globalised. It is being taken out of its traditional context and disseminated by new media of communication.

In the global age, the scholar's space is opening beyond the traditional spaces of the library, the seminar room and the study into a virtual level. The new technologies of communication have made feasible the virtual university. Whether this is the negation of the idea of the university or a new level of reality with which we have to live will be debated for some time..." Why does the advent of globalisation upset this way of conceptualizing our societies and more specifically, the world of higher education?

Essentially, because globalisation is a social process that radically redefines the space for any form of social action and where the compression of time shakes up our notions of the action's place and territory, thereby undermining their reality.

From my standpoint, this illustrious globalisation is structured by three factors. First, the loosening of the territorial attachment of the action, whether this be political, economic, educational, social, cultural, etc.; and, second, the creation of a new global space within which new global issues crystallize.

The third and last factor is the role of this new space as the new forum for the confrontation and negotiation of collective preferences whose mission is to define this new global space. Expressed differently, globalisation is first and foremost an entire redefinition by the actors of their space for taking action. This quest obviously does not take place in a social vacuum. It is characterized by the emergence of new issues and the implementation of new rules and standards that will provide this global space with an orderly structure.

The globalized world is one that can only be built by eliminating a non-negligible portion of the rules respected until now.". Stated in this manner, globalisation is not to be understood as a mere continuation of internationalization. Internationalization takes into account the state of exchanges and flows that occur between dispersed entities; for instance, the foreign trade between two countries, or the exchanges of students and professors between universities. Two major social phenomena, or two major changes, have favoured its emergence. The first originates in the fact that our societies are now organized around knowledge production, having evolved from an industrial development mode into a communications development mode.

The immediate consequence of such evolution is that industrial goods no longer constitute the driving force behind economic activity, while the creation of new knowledge products are defining the capacity for innovation in socio-economics. Because of this transition, knowledge has undergone a change in status and has become a commodity that is bought and sold, exported and imported like any other product.

The impact this has on university communities is momentous.The key factor to bear in mind, however, is that in this knowledge-based society, universities have lost their monopoly over the production and distribution of knowledge. Moreover, the presence of other market players now enjoying this same production capacity is leading to new university-institution-business partnerships or strategic alliances. Finally, this has also led to a restructuring of research activities in universities around initiatives that are directly transferable to and profitable in the marketplace, all at the expense of other research whose focus is more long-term and whose economic impact is therefore more remote.

In other words, these transformations potentially herald the coming of a new modus operandi in university communities, creating new stresses and fragmentation, and these must be assessed and understood. New information technologies and their accelerated development obviously constitute the second factor that has contributed to the development of globalisation in university communities.

Universities will be forced into making basic decisions in the near future as a result of the impact of information and communication technologies (ICTs) on research and teaching activities, their deterritorialization as well as their networking, the emerging e-learning global market and the presence of new players on this scene, and the creation of virtual universities, all in the context of a North-South digital fracture. Finally, these transformations, which are clothed in a reductive, trickle-down discourse on globalisation seeking to make the marketplace the organizational focus for all life in society, have contributed to the emergence of practices and a mercantile discourse in universities which proposes the conquest of the education market as the only viable strategy.

Furthermore, it is not unthinkable that the current round of World Trade Organization negotiations dealing with the General Agreement on Trades in Services

(GATS) and the creation of the Free Trade Area of the Americas (FTAA), including removal of tariff barriers in the world of education, is a major issue that points to the direction of this mercantilization of higher education. We will have more to say about this further on. These transitions are such that while they make globalisation more imposing, they also create new critical issues for universities. The first one involves the knowledge gap between universities in developed countries and those in emerging countries which has been widening continuously since the early 1980s.

The past twenty years have seen an increase in the number of students attending universities world-wide but also widening gaps between the percentages of young people studying in emerging countries versus those in developed countries. In addition, while there was one doctoral graduate per 5,000 inhabitants in OECD countries in 1997, there was only one per 70,000 in Brazil, one per 140,000 in Chile and one per 770,000 in Columbia.

In a world dominated by new knowledge production, such statistics understandably become a source of concern regarding the possibility of emerging countries to successfully integrate into this new economy. The second major issue in the world of higher education is the brain drain from emerging countries to developed countries, an issue that university authorities will soon have to confront.

The global demographic context, indicating relatively aging developed societies compared with very young emerging societies cannot by itself explain and justify this situation. Brainpower and expertise are the raw materials that nurture the knowledge-based economy. Stated rather bluntly, we must ask ourselves if after having guaranteed the growth of developed countries following World War II by what some have called the plundering of natural resources in countries of the South, will developed countries now in the early 21 st century go south once again to loot these countries of their intellectual elite?

The entire problem resides in the relationships between these national systems in regulating higher education while dealing with the global issues discussed earlier. In other words, we are raising the question of an institutional deficit in the global space of higher education. If globalisation in no way lends itself to being reduced to its sole economic dimension and even less to that of a neo-liberal project, this must not blind us to the hegemony of the so-called neo-liberal project in the organization of new global spaces.

Contrary to what a quick analysis of the globalisation situation may lead one to believe, when faced with the question "What to do" regarding globalisation, more than one answer comes to mind. As regards higher education, it should be noted that there are also highly diversified proposals as to the organization and operating principles underlying this global university space.

To begin with, there is a serious trend towards the commercialization and privatization of higher education via the importing of an entrepreneurial management and culture into the universities themselves, but also through the appearance of new private entrepreneurs who, under the university label, are offering educational products on the world market of higher education. This observation cannot be sidestepped: the spatial restructuring of university actions is accompanied by a market culture that has university institutions exporting knowledge, selling or marketing their expertise, opening campus subsidiaries abroad, developing market opportunity strategies for winning over foreign students, reducing students to the status of client, all within a more general context of reducing tariff barriers and a significant reduction in the State's participation in financing universities.

The negotiation of the very definition of this concept, its financing, choice of priorities and ways and means for collective actions, co-ordinating public and private actors, all raise even more critical and highly challenging issues involving the re-legitimization of international public intervention and the need for going beyond the current intergovernmental framework.

The enshrinement of higher education in a global project for sustainable human development that would answer the needs of present generations without compromising the capacities of future generations, or even the conception of universities as central vectors for the interconnections between societies also constitute other proposals for organizing this global space. Obviously, we must draw up the widest range of possibilities for the organizational modelling of the global space occupied by higher education.

Nonetheless, this short and non-exhaustive list that has been presented here demonstrates that the debate is now open and that the idea of structuring global space beyond the nation-state-implementing a suitable institutional architecture that will make it possible to democratically define all the processes for decision-making, assessing and legitimizing collective choices within the global space of higher education-quite likely constitutes the most important impact of globalisation on academia. This is the most important impact of globalisation on universities: this order that beckons us to rethink the world of higher education and make universities participate in building a democratic and equitable world to live in.

After the decay of a 'universal' church and its notion of a supra-national authority in the Renaissance, most universities were in fact founded by states to serve national interests. With the beginning of the new millennium, however, such national definitions are increasingly under attack or simply dissolve under pressures of growing competition and globalisation. Suddenly, universities are supposed to serve not just as "custodians of the genius of nations" but also "active instruments of national competitiveness".

With the technological advances of transportation and information, scholarly and scientific contacts have multiplied and intensified. Students and information can travel quickly and cheaply between countries.

Furthermore, after decades of efforts of internationalisation by idealistic individuals and progressive institutions, internationalisation has now become a key entrepreneurial arena in some countries, international student flows are being marketed, knowledge, in the form of skilled human resources, science, technology, research products, has become a vital resource for industrialised countries. When talking about international cooperation, the term internationalisation often appears as a synonym for international cooperation.

In light of the many different reflected and non-reflected uses of the terms internationalisation, globalisation and Europeanisation, our first step has to consist in some terminological clarifications. In the simplest sense, internationalisation refers to the sum of all those activities which aim to expand their reach over national borders.

The process of integrating the international dimension into teaching, research and service functions of an institution of higher education, an international dimension referring to a perspective, activity or programme which introduces or integrates an international, intercultural or global outlook into the major functions of the institution. Another more selective understanding of the term emphasises "the process of systematic integration of an international dimension into the teaching, research and public service function of a higher education institution".

In this sense, not many institutions which are active in international cooperation could be said to engage in internationalisation although, as we will point out later, a trend towards such systematic integration of an international dimension activities is clearly observable. Globalisation refers to "forceful changes in the economic, social, political and cultural environment" brought about by global competition, the integration of markets, increasingly dense communication networks, information flows and mobility.

Reflecting processes of global competitiveness, for example between great regional blocs such as the United States, the European Union and the Pacific Rim, implies, as Peter Scott formulates, a radical reordering of the old world-order of Great Powers since "national boundaries are rendered obsolete by the transgressive tendencies of high technology and mass culture". Globalisation should not be confused with or simply regarded as a higher form of internationalisation for three reasons: while internationalisation presupposes the notion of nation states and is often conditioned by geo-political concerns, globalisation ignores or transcends the order of nation states altogether.

Secondly, internationalisation processes are often owned, initiated and expressed by the "'high' worlds of diplomacy and culture" while globalisation belongs to the "'low' worlds of mass consumerism and global capitalism".

Thirdly, depending on the unequal pattern of nation states, internationalisation tends to reproduce hierarchy and hegemony while globalisation processes can bring up new agendas beyond existing hierarchies. Globalisation poses a fundamental challenge to tertiary education both with respect to the core functions of the university and to its institutional self-definition.

For the purposes of our study, we see globalisation as the uncontrollable processes of dissolving national boundaries and hegemony brought about by world competition and the integration of markets both of which have been made possible by high technology. In contrast, internationalisation we regard as the active response of a given institution of higher education to the perceived insufficiencies of national definitions of the core functions of higher education.

Since globalisation processes have often sharpened the perception of such insufficiencies among university representatives, internationalisation activities can in many cases even be regarded as institutional responses to globalisation processes. But while the latter ignore national boundaries, internationalisation works with them in order to transcend them. Europeanisation, in the context of this study, we will simply regard as a geographical subset of internationalisation.

In spite of the different political aims which are associated with its funding and the complex processes of regional integration and redistribution of power implied in the term, it has been shown that in most cases, the aims and handling of European cooperation activities at institutional level do not differ significantly from the rest of international cooperation activities and can be seen to contribute to internationalisation at large.

Ironically, as the European Union, while talking about Europe, is a powerful actor of internationalisation, whereby Europe is actually predominantly a sub-category of less than systematic relevance.

Most European countries have known the influx of students from their former colonies. Large numbers of Latin American students seek to obtain postgraduate degrees in Northern American universities.

In the heights of the Cold War the higher education institutions of the Soviet Union and Eastern European countries attracted students from ideologically associated nations.

Furthermore, educational exchange between the US and Western Europe after 1945 was developed to foster democracy and develop the Atlantic community. Generally, geopolitical considerations always have been influential in policies regarding student mobility. However, there is also a growing conviction that one of the most effective means to prepare future graduates for the needs of an increasingly international professional life in a global economy is simply to study and live abroad.

The educational and social benefits, such as acquiring new and cross-cultural knowledge and competencies, improving foreign language proficiency (especially in English), establishing international personal and professional networks, becoming familiar with other countries and cultures, etc. are being stressed by international educators.

In addition, broad cultural values such as internationalism in itself, the belief that cross-cultural educational and scientific exchange is a good in itself or that it promotes also the international understanding and cross-cultural sensitivity among home students and the wider community, go hand in hand with more economic considerations such as the broadening of educational markets and the generation of extra income. Unlike the more marginal student mobility flows of earlier times, international student flows have now become a central feature of the global higher education system. Their quantitative development is impressive.

Over the past forty years the world-wide growth rates in international student flows outweighed even the expansion rates of higher education in general, which underwent massification especially after the seventies. Recently, it seems that the number of foreign students in relative terms, i.e. measured as a percentage of the entire world student population, is actually on the decrease. This appears less surprising if one takes into account the massive expansion of higher education even on a global scale, which has now superseded the rise of foreign students.

According to UNESCO statistics, there were some 1.5 million foreign students in the top 50 host countries in 1994-95. Over the last 25 years international student mobility has risen by more than 300%. Most individual countries witness substantial growth rates of foreign student enrolment.

Many observers expect its growth to continue for awhile, even if the annual growth rates will diminish gradually. Some prognoses make mention of 2.8 million students studying abroad world-wide by 2010 and 4.9 million by 2025, with the by far biggest expansion rates occurring in Asia from where 2.9 million students studying abroad are estimated to proceed in 2025.

The imbalance of receiving and sending students seems to increase. As receiving countries the Anglo-Saxonhigher education systems attract by far the most significant shares. With respect to the mentioned exponentially increasing shares of students from Asia, for example, the USA alone receives nearly double as many students (291,000) as European countries do (170,500).

In fact, Asian students constitute about well over half of all foreign students in the US. Of the share of Asian students hosted in the EU, about three fifths target the UK. Currently, about one third of the student mobility flows of the world are received by the US (nearly 500,000), a share which the president, secretary of state and the secretary of education of the United States are eager to augment. Australia has been greatly increasing its share of incoming students from abroad.

In one decade the number of foreign students enrolled at Australian universities has tripled. Europe occupies a rather unusual position as compared with other industrialised countries: While Europe hosts about half of all foreign students (51%), more than half of these students also originate from other European countries.

In Europe, where numbers in organised mobility are probably highest world-wide, the percentage of organised mobility probably does not exceed 20%. When talking about conditions of student mobility programmes we should keep this fact in mind, especially as we turn to the possible future courses of action which should take account of these less controllable more market-oriented flows. If we turn now to the small but significant share of international student mobility which is supported and stimulated by various kinds of programmes and schemes, it should be noted that most countries have a variety of bilateral and multilateral agreements and programmes in this field.

One of the best known programmes of international student mobility is the European ERASMUS and subsequent SOCRATES programme. Started in 1987 with a view towards the common market of 1992, ERASMUS had the ambition, among other goals, to increase significantly the mobility of students - 10% of the overall student population were targeted to have studied abroad at least once for a term, semester of year during their degree courses in order to develop the European dimension of higher education and to strengthen a European social identity.

Such immersion in other European contexts was seen to support the creation of an internal market of professionals and qualified workers. Since prior to Maastricht the European Commission had no explicit competencies in education and direct strategies at harmonisation of the structures of higher education were considered to be beyond its political competence, student mobility was the vehicle of a strategy of Europeanisation of higher education. Within less than ten years it reached the level of more than 100,000 mobile European students a year and with this result it was considered to be one of the most successful European programmes in the field of education, even if the original target of giving 10% of all EC-students the opportunity to study abroad was not reached.

To some extent, the success of ERASMUS / SOCRATES is of course also due to supportive national policies of member states, providing additional funding. ERASMUS and SOCRATES are not the sole, perhaps not even the most important frameworks of international student mobility in the world.

In the Asia/Pacific region the "University Mobility in Asia and the Pacific" programme (UMAP), established in 1991, is important although it has not yet resulted in some kind of funding scheme. Smaller student mobility programmes exist in most world regions. International student mobility increasingly is a regional and not only an intercontinental phenomenon.

Regional economic integration processes also instigate student mobility and international treaties such as NAFTA, ASEAN or APEC have proven to be stimulating in this respect. Changes in development aid policies also tend to stress more regional student mobility than South-North mobility. The ERASMUS / SOCRATES programme in Europe and the UMAP in the Asia-Pacific region are specifically designed to promote regional student mobility.

Of regional nature is also the NORDPLUS-programme of student exchange in the Nordic countries with its original and attractive "money follows student"-imperative. The most important global movement still is that towards the United States, which is the largest receiving country of foreign students with 34% of the OECD-total.

The transatlantic mobility between Europe (and other world regions) and the US for example, implemented on a multilateral and reciprocal basis under the International Student Exchange Program (ISEP), is confronted with an increasing unbalance. American universities have a growing attraction on European students and the growth of intra-European programmes has not negatively affected this, while European universities seem to have lost some of their attractiveness for US-students.

The world-famous top research universities of the US exert an enormous attraction on mobile students all over the world, but also the second rank American universities receive important numbers of foreign students. The dominance of English as the lingua franca in contemporary science and scientific training and the most commonly mastered second language contributes to the fact that besides the US also the UK, Canada and Australia are among the top host countries world-wide.

From the point of view of the countries of origin of mobile students, it is clear that market-driven, economic factors put into the shade older, more traditional links such as (post) colonial relations. It is no wonder that the newly industrialising economies of the Asian and Pacific region are major sources of foreign students, who aspire to fill the ranks of the growing professional classes. The example of Australia shows that the emergence of a more trade-oriented policy towards foreign students, whereby universities engaged in student recruitment and marketing strategies, was a fruitful enterprise at least from a mercantile point of view.

Education is seen by the Australian state as the fastest growing export industry, which was expected to generate an export income of 3.5 billion US$ by the year 2000, hopes which were put on hold due to the Asian-Pacific economic crisis.

The number of full-fee paying international student enrolment rose from 7,131 in 1987 to more than 143,000 full-fee-paying students in 1996 in Australia, including 54,000 at the higher education level. Indeed, international student flows have become "more trade than aid" in many host countries, since often international students are or have become full-fee-paying students.

In many host institutions, especially in Anglo-Saxon countries, the income of fee-paying foreign students is a welcome addition to shrinking domestic funding, without which many departments would be threatened with closure.

Revenue generation has become an important rationale in institutional policies promoting recruitment of foreign students. A growing part of international student mobility thus is becoming market-driven rather than state-driven or aid-oriented. The international market in education services is becoming a booming sector and the international marketing of domestic universities and the recruitment of students are central elements of it.

Some countries are developing well-organised national policies in this field, such as France with its marketing initiative by EduFrance and its 1,058 associations in 132 countries of the Alliance Française, or Great Britain with the "Welcome to the UK" initiative and the British Council's 211 offices in 147 countries. Some countries, such as Canada, Australia, New Zealand and even South Africa after 1994, have developed ambitious strategic plans in order to strengthen their market position in the field.

With the end of the strong expansion at universities, which, after decades of massive expansion, had seemed to most higher education representatives like a kind of "natural" growth, the opposite trend is already being observed in some fields and many countries, namely a growing trend to seek and actively compete for students, also for the sake of maintaining sufficient levels of public funding which is linked to student enrolment in most countries.

In many higher education communities this is something new, which also induces many actors to try and discover new "markets" of potential students. Since one may expect students' choices to increase, institutions of higher education will have to and are beginning to pay more attention to their needs and satisfaction than was customary e.g. in continental Europe in the past.

The distinction line with student mobility is not always very clear due to the large numbers of mobile postgraduate and Ph.D. students. In many regions and specific areas of study, such as business administration, regional and international training networks for young researchers and professionals have become well-established.

Of course, there is a great deal of "natural" mobility in the academic profession, due to the international character of scientific research and training. Traditionally, international mobility among professors is most often motivated by research and scholarship and is stimulated by the growth of global and increasingly competitive research scenes with its abundant conferences, meetings and joint research projects, but also by the availability of cheap air travel.

Education and teaching have become reasons for international mobility only recently. As with student mobility there is a great deal of geographic inequality in the mobility flows. The International Survey of the Academic Profession has shown a high polarisation between countries with high academic immigration, sometimes as a result of deliberate international recruitment of academic staff for expanding higher education systems, and countries with low levels of internationalisation of faculty. The US and the UK are the major important ex- and importers of academic labour, but compared to the domestic production of highly skilled academics the picture is much more diverse.

Developing countries and Eastern European countries face the problem of emigration of researchers and academic staff to the global centres of research. A massive problem of brain drain therefore exists on a global scale at the expense of developing and "second world" regions.

Accordingly, more and more representatives of the labour markets and higher education institutions see the need to integrate foreign languages and courses on foreign cultures, politics and legal frameworks into existing curricula.

Furthermore, the political integration process in the European Union has fostered the desire to support the construction of a European citizenship and social identity with European studies elements in relevant disciplines, in addition to the additional knowledge of the framework conditions of a European labour market. However, the respect of the variety of national systems of higher education and the subsidiary powers of governments and institutions with regard to curricula has often dampened the aspiration to de-nationalise curricula.

In Europe, the de-nationalisation of curricula was viewed with such mistrust - especially by member state authorities who feared that their competence was being encroached upon—that the introduction of European elements into existing curricula could only be realised by means of mobility projects.

This was one of the reasons why the management of mobility programmes was situated at the level of the departments and not, as in the American examples, at the level of the institutions and their central international offices. Nevertheless, there are some meaningful developments towards international curricula in various countries and regions. Internationalising curricula can also be seen as something more comprehensive than developing curricula with international components, namely the international harmonisation of curricula.

The most powerful inducement to internationalise curricula has probably come from the growing impact of international professional associations. The rapid growth in international trade in professional services has provoked several professions to organise themselves at an international scale.

These international professional associations started to deal with issues of education and training, such as quality assurance, international minimum standards, criteria of professionalism, accreditation, etc. and usually promote the greater convergence of curricula and quality criteria. Some professions have been very active in this matter, such as the engineering, the medical or the legal professions.

Professional associations, organised at an international level, thus have exerted a harmonising influence on standards and curricula in view of the professional accreditation of programmes and the professional recognition of degrees in various countries. In some instances, these international professional standards are legally enforced by international organisations.

The European Union for example increasingly deals with minimum standards of education and training in view of the mobility of labour and the recognition of entry into specific professions in the common market.

Also organisations such as OECD and WTO are becoming increasingly interested in these matters and free trade agreements such as NAFTA or ASEAN often contain clauses on mutual recognition of licensing or certification procedures in view of the international mobility of professional services.

Institutions of higher education are now challenged to introduce meaningful first degrees which are shorter, more flexible (through the adoption of credit systems), more relevant to professional life, more multidisciplinary, more European and international, as well as to create masters degrees in environments where there were no short, or separate, programmes at this level in order to meet the needs and expectations of the mobile students from the rest of Europe and the world.

The main benefit one would expect from the development of such independent master's courses would be to have a much wider redistribution of students entering the postgraduate level than we currently have, which could also pave the way for a new type of mobility.

Most remarkably perhaps, the Bologna Declaration signals a political turning point in the history of cooperation in higher education since it constitutes a pledge freely taken by the 29 signatory countries to reform their own systems in such a way that its structures may converge clearly and thus constitutes a dramatic shift away from the generally hesitant and reactive role which the member states of the EU used to play in a political scene of university cooperation which was most often fuelled by initiatives of the European Commission.

In the US, the Association of International Education Administrators (AIEA), in cooperation with national academic associations, published very influential Guidelines for International Education at US Colleges and Universities already in 1983 which called for the establishment of one central institutional "lead point", a senior administrator with the responsibility "for developing strategy and managing activities tied to internationalising the institution."

In Europe, the European Commission revised the managerial framework of its successful ERASMUS programme in 1994 in order to enhance institutional commitment and foster the central administration's involvement and support of European cooperation. Accordingly, ERASMUS/SOCRATES now requires that higher education institutions collect the whole array of European cooperation activities under the framework of one institutional application and formulate a "European Policy Statement" every three years explaining the status and context of their planned cooperation activities. Only in a few European countries, such internationalisation statements were already established practice.

The majority of higher education institutions formulated such a policy statement for the first time and did not just adapt an already existing policy statement for the purpose.

As recent studies have shown, these new requirements have indeed contributed to lending greater visibility and transparency to internationalisation issues and practice in the eyes of the central administration and decision-making bodies, leading in many cases to increased support and coordination of exchange services, institution-wide recognition guidelines and mobilisation of hitherto inactive areas.

It is generally agreed that it makes a great difference whether the initiative for internationalisation proceeds from a component of the institution, such as a department or research group, or whether the institution's internationalisation is also being initiated, coordinated, planned and systematically integrated by the institution's central leadership. Of course, institutional contexts in which international cooperation activities are being undertaken vary greatly.

Many higher education institutions are currently moving into this crucial phase of institutionalisation, often helped or propelled into it by support from funding schemes.

In the past decade, the quality of educational provision has become an increasingly urgent concern in most countries. The growing urgency with which the issue of quality has been dealt with among higher education representatives but also among politicians and government officials and other stakeholders can be attributed to a number of factors.

First of all, as van Damme points out, the massification of higher education has exerted increasing pressure on infrastructures as well as on human and financial resources and has heightened the need for efficient expenditure.

Secondly, key stakeholders, businesses, professional bodies and employer organisations have voiced their concern about the capacities of traditional academic management to guarantee adequate quality standards and to respond to the needs of modern work places and labour markets in an increasingly competitive and transformative economy.

Thirdly, in most industrialised countries, budget restrictions and fiscal crises have led to a decrease in government funding per student and a pressure to increase efficiency in public expenditure.

Fourthly, the deregulation of many national higher education system has not only increased institutional autonomy but also the demands of the "evaluative state" and public accountability. The establishment of quality assurance policies and mechanisms in many countries took place in a political and governmental environment characterised by a changing relationship between the state and the institutional field. Especially in Western Europe, deregulation, increasing institutional autonomy, devolution of authority, a shifting balance between state- and market-oriented elements in the steering of higher education systems, and a growing weight of output-related, performance-based factors in steering and sometimes also financing, were the decisive features of that changing relationship.

Governments converted their higher education policies from an input-oriented regulation into an output-oriented steering. In general, there was an exchange between deregulation and institutional autonomy on the one hand and quality assurance, accountability and output-control on the other hand. Furthermore, increasing mobility of students who do not only want to study abroad but also want to have these studies recognised upon return, as well as the heightened opportunities of students to move to places and institutions which they perceive to best respond to their needs, have highlighted the importance of quality assurance and improvement.

Finally, the growth of competition from private providers which respond to market needs more flexibly have raised concerns of consumer protection, minimum quality standards and the protection of fundamental academic values.

In Eastern Europe, for example, the development of quality assurance and accreditation schemes can to a large extent be attributed to the increasingly complex situation caused by the establishment of numerous private higher education institutions.

In the relationship between internationalisation and the quality of higher education three different dimensions can be distinguished:

— the contribution of internationalisation to the improvement of the quality of higher education;

— the quality of internationalisation as such;

— the international dimension of quality assurance systems and mechanisms in higher education.

Increasingly, new technologies are used to complement and support established cooperation activities, be it mobility or curriculum development.

A number of "administrative" examples may serve to illustrate the use of satellites, the Internet, and the World Wide Web in higher education cooperation, such as statistical databases to track students and their progress; Web pages to introduce study abroad options, including detailed information on course work and living situations; the use of e-mail to receive and submit assignments as well as communicate with individual tutors or remain in touch with home students and professors; and online applications to support classroom teaching, providing convenience and saving time. Two broad categories of usage seem to encompass the majority of applications: courses offered over the Internet and the World Wide Web, focusing primarily on students; and research collaboration, focusing on faculty. The number of courses offered electronically is increasing rapidly.

Many of these are prepared and delivered by individual faculty, but often entire units of an institution or indeed entire institutions are being established to offer online alternatives. Especially in the US, the offer of complete degree programmes is available in a growing range of disciplines.

Traditional universities are also beginning to offer complete degree programmes online. In this new environment, new organisations also emerge, e.g. brokerage organisations, such as the Globewide Network Academy and the Electronic University Network, which help link students with institutions offering courses online, as well as organisations which develop their own courses. Indeed, with the expansion of the new technologies, a considerable growth of new providers of higher education services can be noted, adding to the choice available to students and to the concerns about minimum quality standards.

upsurge of interest in accreditation in many countries can be linked to these concerns and to the desires of new institutions to receive marketable labels. Indeed, more and more universities of the industrialised world, mostly in Anglo-Saxon countries which tend to adopt a more market-oriented, entrepreneurial approach to the recruitment of students, are not satisfied by the increasing numbers of mobile students coming to them.

They combine recruitment of foreign students with extending their educational supply to promising markets in other countries by setting up local campuses under the full authority of the mother institution. Complete programmes from commencement through graduation are possible in this system, if the local state legally permits the granting of foreign diplomas and degrees on its territory.

Information and communication technologies through the Internet and satellite transmission open up avenues of developments in educational delivery modes in which geographical limitations are eliminated. As van Damme observes, "some see the future of global higher education in the emergence of a limited number of global virtual universities, designed by powerful corporations; others think of most current universities providing higher education as well through traditional delivery modes as through virtual modes or, which is highly probable, various intermediate modes."

Education and Globalisation

Globalisation, describes the spread of industrialisation from one country to another. But, what is spread are innovations that depend increasingly upon more or less specialised knowledge inputs and this, in turn, is driven by competition between firms. The presence of static competition drives a firm's to search for efficiency gains by constantly trying to improve the ways in which existing resources are allocated.

At this level, the discovery process often involves a degree of R&D activity, sometimes with universities, as firms seek to improve the industrial processes they have adopted and performance characteristics of the products that they currently make.

The result is a stream of incremental innovations within the framework a previously chosen set of technologies; what is often described as a design configuration. At the level of static competition, markets operate to choose amongst products and because firms differ in the efficiency with which they operate, there results in each sector, a hierarchy of firms distributed about what is sometimes referred to as "average best practice". Under dynamic competition, things are very different.

Dynamic competition also launches a discovery process but in a different form, in the sense that it is a search for novel design configurations—novel combinations of scientific ideas and technologies—that might form the bases for the long term survival of the firm, should its existing set of technologies—its current design configuration—be attacked by innovations from one quarter or another.

In other words, dynamic competition launches the sort of search behaviour that firms undertake in anticipation of the possibility that from somewhere a knowledge solution will arise which might render their current technological base and associated work force obsolete.

But since it is not known what these knowledge solutions will be or where such they may arise from, firms deal with this type of risk by participating in joint activities, often joint research activities. To accomplish this, they join networks, enter alliances and form partnerships of various kinds. In terms of the search process, these collaborations form complex problem-solving sites. Solutions are pursued collaboratively, involving many participants, and, paradoxically, they often involve competitors.

Under dynamic competition, markets operate not to choose between products for there are none yet, but between research groups. And, because groups differ in their creativity, the performance of each research group will depend on its composition. It is, therefore, of the utmost importance for firms which, and how many, research collaborations they join.

Globalisation is, in part, about the imitation and adaptation of these "knowledge solutions" as they diffuse from one firm to another and from country to another. For the purposes of this exposition, the main point to note that globalisation because it stimulates dynamic competition drives the proliferation of collaborative problem solving sites as it draws more and more firms into its competitive ambit. The evidence for this is unequivocal: the numbers of these collaborative ventures are expanding exponentially across a large number of sectors.

Of course, the human resources for these collaborative research ventures are drawn the employees of firms, but they also make use of the expertise that lies in a socially distributed knowledge production system which is rapidly acquiring a global dimension. Now, these sites of collaborative research function as "attractors" for the academic community, in part because in many cases they involve research at the leading edge of a disciplinary field, but also because, for many academics, the opportunity to work in these problems solving groups provides an important way for them to utilise and develop their specialist skills.

The spread of globalisation is accompanied by the proliferation of collaborative research arrangements and these ventures are the sites in which new research practices are being developed. Into this process are drawn an increasing number of members of the academic community.

In fact, the numbers of academics participating in this type of industry-driven search for involved are already large enough for the experience to begin to "feedback" into, and so affect, the ways in which research is pursued in universities. Globalisation, through the tensions that it introduces into academic life, is touching the nature of the university at its heart: in the research process itself. It should be noted that, so far at least, the drift of academic researchers into collaborative research with industry has not been the outcome of governmental policy or institutional strategy.

The decisions of academics to join these types of collaborative research activities has been largely a matter of individual choice. It is what academics seem to want to do; and, it must be said, it is often an attractive option for the best of them. If the universities wish to adjust to these changes in the behaviour of their researches - and it is hard to imagine how they might resist - then they need to modify their recruitment policies, their terms and conditions of work and their reward structures. But the consequence of such modifications have profound implications for universities as institutions.

By becoming so deeply involved in the innovation process, universities are being drawn ineluctably closer to industry. But, in doing this, or allowing it to happen, they are in fact also changing the basis of their relationship with the wider society. They need to take their participation in collaborative research beyond the limited business/economic context of the search for novel design configurations. They need to develop the procedures, organisational forms and reward structures that will produce a types of science (and scientists) that are sensitive to context, that takes the search for knowledge solutions beyond a dialogue of experts and that embraces wider social participation in the research process.

Almost everybody sees education as essential to development, but until recently very few of those responsible for formulating education policy for the developing world have acknowledged the value of higher education. This is one of several contradictions that characterize higher education and higher education policy in developing countries, and an example of what I'm going to focus on today.

Education is always given a prominent position in lists of development goals, but higher education is almost never mentioned. Organizations like the World Bank have traditionally accorded higher education a very low priority, believing both that it favored the elite in society and that returns on higher education investment were much lower than returns on investment in primary and secondary education.

Higher education is essential to promoting sustainable human development and economic growth. It is no longer a luxury that only rich countries can afford, but an absolute necessity for all countries, and especially for poor countries. The pressures of globalization make it urgent that we devote substantially more resources to the tertiary education sector, and that we also reform it at both the level of individual institutions and the system as a whole.

Bibliography

Bernfeld, S., *Sisyphus or the limits of education* (F.Lilge, trans.), Berkeley: University of California Press, 1973.

L. Lloyd (ed.), *Teaching with Technology, Rethinking Tradition,* Medford, NJ: Information Today, Inc., 2000.

Dewey, J., *Democracy and education,* London: Macmillan, 1916.

Elias N., *The Civilising Process: The History of Manners,* Oxford: Blackwell, 1978.

Freud, A., *Psychoanalysis for teachers and parents* (B. Low, trans.), Boston: Beacon Press, 1935.

Freud, S., "The future of an illusion", In J. Strachey (Ed. and trans.), *The standard edition of the complete psychological works of Sigmund Freud,* London: Hogarth, 1961.

Kuper, W, . 1999. In: *Disadvantage, Dialogue and Development Co-operation in Education.* Report of the IWGE Meeting, June 1998, Munich. Paris, United Nations Educational, Scientific and Cultural Organization/International Institute of Educational Planning.

Malone, T.W., Macken, E., & Suppes, P., *Toward optimal allocation of instructional resources: Dividing computer-assisted instruction time among students,* Instructional Science, 8, 107-20, 1979.

Mc Grath, Simon. 1999. Education, Development and Assistance: The Challenge of the New Millennium. In: K. King and L. Buchert (eds.), *Changing International Aid to Education.* Paris, United Nations Educational, Scientific and Cultural Organization and Geneva, Norrag.

Pike, Graham; Senby, David. *In the Global Classroom.* Books 1 and 2. Toronto, Pippin Publishing, 1998.

Suppes, P., "Can there be a normative philosophy of education? In G.L. Newsome, Jr. (Ed.), Philosophy of Education", *Studies in Philosophy and Education series,* Proceedings of the 24th annual meeting of the Philosophy of Education Society--Santa Monica, April 7-10, 1968.

______________, "The concept of obligation in the context of decision theory", In J. Leach, R. Butts, & G. Pearce (Eds.), Science, decision and value, *Proceedings of the Fifth University of Western Ontario Philosophy Colloquium,* 1969, Dordrecht: Reidel.

______________, "Lorenz curves for various processes: A pluralistic approach to equity", *Social Choice and Welfare,* 5, 89-101, Reprinted in W. Gaertner & P.K. Pattanaik (Eds.), Distributive Justice and Inequality, Berlin Heidelberg: Springer-Verlag, 1-13, 1988.

Tressou, Evangelia. 1977. *Exclusion of Special Groups from Education and through Education: Who is at Risk?* International Conference on Human Dignity and Social Exclusion: Educational Policies in Europe, Athens.

Index